Womanizer

Nail the Women Now!

Ravee Shekhar

Published by: Ravee Shekhar

Printed at: Crownytec Solution

Womanizer- Nail the Women Now!

ISBN: 978-93-342-6223-0

Disclaimer: This book is intended for informational purposes only and does not guarantee success in impressing women. Individual experiences may vary based on personal circumstances, cultural differences, and individual preferences. The strategies and insights provided are not a substitute for genuine connection, respect, and consent in any relationship. Readers are encouraged to approach interactions with authenticity and kindness, recognizing that every individual is unique. The author is not responsible for any outcomes resulting from the application of this content.

Didication

Dedicated to all those Women who have Touched my Heart

Content

Preface

In a world where connections are often fleeting and genuine relationships can feel elusive, the art of impressing women has become a topic of great interest and importance. This book, "Womanizer – Nail the Women Now!" is designed to guide you through the nuances of attraction, communication, and authenticity, helping you navigate the complexities of modern relationship with confidence and grace. You will learn how to impress the Women with Ease. Actually, Impressing Women is Art, Science and Commerce all simultaneously.

Drawing from a wealth of research, personal anecdotes, and insights from relationship experts, this guide aims to demystify the process of making a lasting impression. It is not about adopting a façade or employing manipulative tactics; rather, it emphasizes the value of being your true self while enhancing the qualities that make you unique. The goal is to empower you to forge meaningful connections that are built on mutual respect and understanding.

Throughout these pages, you will discover practical tips and strategies that can be easily integrated into your daily life. From mastering the art of conversation to understanding body language, each chapter is crafted to equip you with the tools necessary to engage with women authentically and effectively. You will learn how to showcase your strengths, embrace vulnerability, and cultivate an aura of confidence that naturally attracts others.

Whether you are seeking to enhance your dating life, build lasting relationships or simply improve your social skills, this book is your companion on the journey to becoming the best version of yourself. Remember, impressing women is not about perfection; it's about connection. So, let's embark on this adventure together, and unlock the secrets to making a genuine impression that resonates long after the first encounter.

Gratitude for all those women who have touched my heart reflects emotional maturity and appreciation for the journey of life. This book is my tribute to the lessons they have taught me.

Ravee Shekhar

RaveeShekhar@yahoo.com

Resolution for the Readers

"If you can't give Happiness

to Someone, You also don't

have the right to give

them Sorrow."

Introduction

A Journey of Being Womanizer – The Allen's Story

Allen sat on a park bench, the sun casting a warm glow over the vibrant autumn leaves. He watched couples stroll by, hand in hand, laughter echoing in the air. As he sipped his coffee, he couldn't help but feel a pang of longing. Despite his good nature and sense of humor, he often found himself struggling to connect with women. He had been on countless dates, but none had blossomed into something meaningful. Frustrated yet hopeful, he decided it was time for a change.

One evening, while scrolling through his favorite bookstore's website, Allen stumbled upon this book. Intrigued, he read the description: a guide to Impressing Women with ease, understanding women's emotions, building confidence, and fostering genuine connections. It promised to be a roadmap for navigating the complexities of attraction and relationships. With a sense of determination, he ordered the book, eager to embark on a journey of self-discovery and growth.

The First Chapter: Understanding Women's Emotions as Allen delved into the first chapter, he was captivated by the exploration of the psychology behind attraction and affection. He learned that attraction is not merely about physical appearance; it is deeply rooted in emotional connection. The chapter emphasized the importance of emotional intelligence - understanding and empathizing with women's feelings. Allen realized that he had often overlooked this crucial aspect in his interactions.

He recalled a recent date where he had been so focused on impressing his date with witty banter that he failed to notice her subtle cues of discomfort. The book encouraged him to practice active listening and to genuinely engage with women's emotions. Inspired, Allen made a commitment to himself: he would strive to understand the feelings of the women he met, creating a foundation for deeper connections.

Building Confidence and Charisma With newfound insights, Allen moved on to Chapter 2, which focused on building confidence and charisma. He learned that self-confidence is magnetic; it draws people in and creates an inviting atmosphere. The chapter provided practical techniques to boost his self-esteem, such as positive affirmations and setting small, achievable goals.

Allen had always struggled to connect with women, often misreading their signals. One evening, he stumbled upon a Chapter 3, about body language and as he delved into its pages, everything changed. He learned to recognize the subtle cues of interest and disinterest, transforming his approach to interactions. Suddenly, conversations felt more fluid; he could sense when a woman was engaged or pulling away. Armed with this newfound knowledge, Allen approached social situations with confidence, no longer second-guessing himself. As he navigated relationships with clarity, he discovered deeper connections, ultimately reshaping his understanding of attraction and communication.

Allen began to implement these techniques in his daily life. He started dressing more intentionally, choosing outfits that made him feel good about himself. He practiced good posture and maintained eye contact during conversations, which helped him project confidence. As he embraced these changes, he noticed a shift in how others responded to him. He felt more at ease in social situations, and his interactions became more engaging.

The Art of Effective Communication Eager to continue his journey, Allen dove into Chapter 3, which emphasized the art of effective communication. He learned that active listening is essential for building rapport and connection. The chapter encouraged him to ask open-ended questions and show genuine interest in others' stories.

One day, while attending a friend's gathering, Allen put his newfound skills to the test. He struck up a conversation with a woman named Sarah, who was passionate about photography. Instead of dominating the conversation, he listened intently, asking questions that encouraged her to share her experiences. As she spoke, he felt a genuine connection forming, and he realized that his active listening made her feel valued.

Mastering the First Impression As Allen progressed through the book, he reached Chapter 4, which focused on mastering the first impression. He learned that body language, eye contact, and personal presentation play a significant role in how others perceive him. The chapter provided practical tips for starting conversations and keeping them interesting.

Armed with this knowledge, Allen approached a new woman at a local art exhibit. He remembered to smile, maintain eye contact, and engage her in conversation about the artwork. Instead of relying on rehearsed lines, he asked her opinion about a particular piece, which sparked a lively discussion. He felt a sense of ease and confidence that he had never experienced before.

Building Deep Connections With each chapter, Allen felt himself growing more confident and self-aware. Chapter 5 focused on building deep connections by understanding a woman's likes, dislikes, and passions. He learned that sharing dreams and aspirations could foster intimacy without coming across as boastful.

During a coffee date with Sarah, he took the opportunity to share his passion for writing. He spoke about his aspirations and the stories he wanted to tell. To his delight, Sarah opened up about her own dreams of becoming a professional photographer. Their conversation flowed effortlessly, and Allen felt a sense of connection that he had longed for.

The Role of Humor and Playfulness In Chapter 6, Allen discovered the importance of humor and playfulness in relationships. He learned that laughter could create comfort and intimacy, making interactions more enjoyable. The chapter encouraged him to embrace light-hearted teasing and playful banter.

During a casual outing with Sarah, Allen decided to incorporate humor into their interactions. He shared funny anecdotes from his life, and they both laughed heartily. The playful atmosphere allowed them to relax and enjoy each other's company, deepening their connection.

As Allen continued his journey through the book, he reached Chapter 7, which emphasized the importance of being genuine and authentic in relationships. He learned that honesty and sincerity are the cornerstones of meaningful connections. The chapter warned against manipulation and playing games, encouraging him to be transparent about his intentions.

Reflecting on his past experiences, Allen realized that he had sometimes tried to present a version of himself that he thought would be more appealing. However, he now understood that true attraction comes from being authentic. He made a conscious decision to embrace his true self in all his interactions, allowing his personality to shine through without fear of judgment.

During a dinner date with Sarah, Allen felt a wave of vulnerability wash over him. He decided to share a personal story about a challenge he had faced in his life. As he spoke openly about his struggles, he noticed Sarah's expression soften. She appreciated his honesty and reciprocated by sharing her own experiences. This moment of vulnerability deepened their connection, and Allen felt a sense of relief in being his true self.

As Allen progressed to Chapter 8, he learned about the inevitability of rejection in dating and how to handle it gracefully. The chapter emphasized that rejection is not a reflection of one's worth but rather a part of the journey toward finding the right connection. It encouraged him to view setbacks as opportunities for growth.

One evening, after a particularly promising date with Sarah, Allen received a text from her expressing that she didn't feel a romantic spark. Initially, he felt a pang of disappointment, but he remembered the lessons from the book. Instead of dwelling on the rejection, he took a moment to reflect on the positive aspects of their time together. He appreciated the connection they had built and recognized that not every interaction would lead to romance.

With a newfound sense of resilience, Allen responded to Sarah with grace, thanking her for the lovely evening and wishing her well. He felt empowered by his ability to handle rejection maturely, knowing that it was simply a part of the dating landscape.

As he moved into Chapter 9, Allen began to think about the future and what it would take to build long-term relationships. He learned that keeping the spark alive after the initial excitement fades requires effort and commitment. The chapter emphasized the importance of supporting and motivating each other, as well as dealing with conflicts constructively.

Allen reflected on his interactions with Sarah and how they had both encouraged each other's passions. He realized that fostering a supportive environment was essential for any relationship to thrive. He made a mental note to continue nurturing connections with those he cared about, whether romantic or platonic.

In Chapter 10, Allen uncovers the manipulative tactics of dark psychology, such as providing attention and then suddenly ignoring, which creates emotional turmoil. He learns about

Love Bombing, where overwhelming affection is followed by withdrawal, and Negging, which undermines self-esteem. Understanding emotional push-pull dynamics reveals how instability keeps women hooked. With this newfound knowledge, Allen resolves to build authentic relationships, transforming his interactions and fostering deeper, healthier connections based on mutual respect.

Allen learns to navigate rejection gracefully in Chapter 11, discovering that it doesn't have to diminish his confidence. He realizes that each setback is an opportunity for emotional growth and self-reflection. By embracing rejection as a stepping stone, he transforms his experiences into motivation for self-improvement. Armed with this perspective, Allen becomes more resilient, fostering a positive mindset that empowers him to pursue new opportunities and build stronger connections in his life.

In Chapter 12, Allen discovers that constant self-improvement is the key to becoming the man Sarah can't resist. He learns practical ways to enhance his skills, confidence, and emotional intelligence, ensuring he remains engaging and intriguing. By focusing on personal growth and maintaining her interest over time, Allen transforms himself into a more appealing partner. With this commitment to self-betterment, he not only captivates Sarah but also enriches his own life, fostering a deeper connection between them.

Finally, Allen reached Chapter 13, which provided practical tips and real-life examples of successful and unsuccessful attempts to impress women. The stories shared in this chapter resonated with him, reinforcing the lessons he had learned throughout the book. He appreciated the insights from relationship experts and psychologists, which offered valuable perspectives on attraction and connection.

As he closed the book, Allen felt a sense of accomplishment. He had embarked on a transformative journey, gaining the tools and knowledge to navigate the complexities of dating and relationships. He understood that impressing women was not about superficial tactics but about building genuine connections based on understanding, empathy, and authenticity.

With a renewed sense of purpose, Allen stepped out into the world, ready to embrace new opportunities for connection. He felt more confident, self-aware, and equipped to engage with women in a meaningful way. He knew that the journey would continue, filled with ups and downs, but he was excited to apply what he had learned.

As he walked through the park, he spotted a group of friends laughing together. He felt a sense of belonging and connection to the world around him. Allen was no longer just a passive observer; he was an active participant in the drama of relationships, ready to impress women with ease and authenticity.

With each interaction, he would strive to understand emotions, communicate effectively, and embrace vulnerability. He was determined to build deep connections and navigate the complexities of dating with grace and confidence.

Allen always dreamed of becoming a true womanizer, effortlessly charming and attracting women wherever he went. But confidence, charisma, and the right approach always eluded him - until he discovered the book. This book became his ultimate guide, unlocking the secrets of attraction, emotional connection, and irresistible confidence. With each chapter, Allen mastered The Art of Winning Women Heart. Soon, women were drawn to him naturally, captivated by his newfound aura. His dream was no longer a fantasy - this book transformed him into the man women desired.

Allen's journey had just begun and he was eager to see where it would lead him. Now, it's your turn to master the art!

Chapter 1: Understanding Women's Emotions

Introduction

To win a woman's heart, you must first understand the complex nature of her emotions. Women, like men, desire love, respect, trust, and appreciation. However, their emotional needs are often expressed and perceived differently. Successfully impressing a woman goes beyond mere attraction; it involves building a deep emotional connection where she feels truly understood and appreciated.

The age-old saying, "Men are from Mars, Women are from Venus," highlights the common perception that men and women think and feel differently. While these differences can be overemphasized, there is some truth to the idea that women, generally speaking, are more emotionally expressive and attuned to their own feelings and the feelings of others.

In this chapter, we will explore the psychological foundations of attraction, the importance of emotional intelligence, and how to genuinely understand a woman's emotions to establish a meaningful connection. Each point will be elaborated with real-life examples, practical tips, and exercises that will help you master the art of understanding women's emotions.

Attraction and affection are complex processes shaped by a unique blend of biological, psychological, and social factors. Women often experience and express emotions differently than men, influenced by variations in brain chemistry, hormonal fluctuations, and social conditioning. Understanding these dynamics is crucial for fostering meaningful relationships and building deeper emotional connections. By developing an awareness of the intricacies of women's emotional landscapes, men can navigate their interactions with greater sensitivity and emotional intelligence, leading to more fulfilling and lasting partnerships.

Biological Factors

The Role of Hormones in Emotional Expression

Women's emotional responses are deeply influenced by hormones such as estrogen, progesterone, and oxytocin. These hormones not only regulate mood and emotional stability but also impact bonding, trust, and intimacy in relationships.

- **Estrogen:** This hormone plays a vital role in mood regulation, influencing emotional sensitivity and responsiveness. Higher estrogen levels often correlate with heightened emotional awareness and expression.
- **Oxytocin:** Known as the "love hormone," oxytocin fosters emotional bonding and trust. It is released during moments of intimacy, such as hugging, kissing, or deep conversations, strengthening the emotional connection between partners.
- **Progesterone:** This hormone influences calmness and relaxation but fluctuates throughout the menstrual cycle, sometimes leading to mood shifts.

By acknowledging these biological underpinnings, men can approach relationships with greater sensitivity, recognizing that women's emotional responses may be influenced by physiological changes rather than purely situational factors.

How Brain Chemistry Affects Emotional Processing

The female brain tends to have a more active limbic system, the part responsible for emotional processing, leading to heightened emotional awareness and empathy. This biological distinction explains why women often display greater emotional intelligence, nurturing tendencies, and a stronger ability to read social cues. Understanding this difference helps men appreciate why women are often more in tune with emotional nuances and interpersonal dynamics.

Psychological Factors

Emotional Security and the Need for Stability

Women tend to prioritize emotional security in their relationships. This need for emotional stability stems from evolutionary psychology, where reliable, supportive partners historically increased survival chances. Consequently, women are naturally drawn to men who demonstrate consistency, emotional availability, and empathy.

Research suggests that women often assess a partner's emotional intelligence and reliability before investing in a relationship. Traits such as attentiveness, dependability, and effective communication play a crucial role in attraction and long-term compatibility.

The Power of Intuition and Emotional Awareness

Studies indicate that women possess higher levels of emotional intelligence than men, making them more intuitive in recognizing and interpreting emotions. This ability allows them to assess nonverbal cues, detect underlying feelings, and respond with empathy.

Men who develop their emotional awareness can create stronger connections by:

- Actively listening without interrupting or offering premature solutions.
- Expressing their own emotions openly and honestly.
- Demonstrating patience and understanding during emotional conversations.

Social and Cultural Influences

Cultural expectations significantly shape how women express their emotions. Many societies encourage women to embody nurturing, empathetic, and emotionally open traits, while men are often socialized to adopt a stoic demeanor. Recognizing these societal norms allows men to approach women with patience and empathy, rather than frustration or confusion. By understanding the cultural context of emotional expression, men can better navigate their interactions with women, fostering an environment of trust and openness that encourages authentic communication.

Emotional Intelligence and Its Importance in Relationships

Emotional intelligence (EQ) is the ability to recognize, understand, and manage emotions in oneself and others. High emotional intelligence is a key factor in building successful relationships, as it fosters empathy, effective communication, and emotional resilience. Men who cultivate their emotional intelligence are better equipped to navigate the complexities of relationships, leading to deeper connections and enhanced satisfaction.

The Four Components of Emotional Intelligence

- **Self-Awareness:** This involves being conscious of one's emotions and understanding how they affect interactions with others. Self-aware individuals can recognize their emotional triggers and respond thoughtfully rather than react impulsively.
- **Self-Regulation:** This component focuses on managing emotions in a way that promotes healthy communication and relationships. Individuals who practice self-regulation can maintain composure during challenging situations, fostering a more constructive dialogue.
- **Social Awareness:** This entails understanding and responding to others' emotions appropriately. Socially aware individuals can pick up on emotional cues, allowing them to connect with others on a deeper level.
- **Relationship Management:** This involves using emotional understanding to build trust and strong connections. Individuals skilled in relationship management can navigate conflicts effectively and foster a supportive environment.

Why Emotional Intelligence Matters

- **Improves Communication:** Women appreciate men who can express themselves clearly and understand emotions without being dismissive. Effective communication fosters a sense of safety and openness in relationships.
- **Enhances Emotional Bonding:** Recognizing emotional cues strengthens trust and intimacy, allowing partners to feel more connected and valued.
- **Helps Resolve Conflicts:** Emotional intelligence facilitates effective conflict resolution, preventing

unnecessary misunderstandings and fostering a collaborative approach to problem-solving.

- **Builds Long-Term Attraction:** Women are often more attracted to men who demonstrate emotional depth and maturity, as these qualities signal stability and reliability in a partner.

How to Genuinely Understand and Empathize with Women's Feelings

The Importance of Active Listening

Listening is more than just hearing words; it involves understanding the emotions behind them. Women feel valued when they are truly heard. Active listening includes:

- **Maintaining Eye Contact:** This shows attentiveness and signals that you are engaged in the conversation.
- **Nodding and Verbal Affirmations:** Simple gestures like nodding and saying "I see" or "I understand" demonstrate engagement and encourage her to share more.
- **Asking Follow-Up Questions:** This shows genuine interest and encourages deeper conversation, allowing her to express her feelings more fully.
- **Summarizing Key Points:** Reflecting back what she has said ensures understanding and validates her emotions.

Validating Her Emotions

Validation is crucial in building emotional security. Instead of dismissing or attempting to fix a woman's concerns, acknowledge her feelings by saying:

- "I understand why you feel that way; it makes sense given the situation."
- "That must have been really difficult for you; I'm here to listen."
- "I can see why that would upset you; your feelings are important." By validating her emotions, you create a safe space for her to express herself, strengthening your emotional connection.

Recognizing Emotional Cues

Women often communicate emotions through body language, tone, and subtle cues. Being observant can help men respond appropriately. Common emotional cues include:

- **Crossed Arms or Averted Gaze:** These may indicate discomfort or irritation, signaling that she may need space or reassurance.
- **Deep Sighs or Quiet Demeanor:** These signs can suggest sadness or exhaustion, prompting a gentle inquiry into her feelings.
- **Excited Speech and Animated Gestures:** These indicate happiness or enthusiasm, providing an opportunity to engage and share in her joy.

Emotional Availability

Being emotionally available means showing genuine interest in her thoughts and feelings. This includes:

- **Being Present During Conversations:** Put away distractions and focus on her, demonstrating that her feelings matter to you.

- **Sharing Personal Emotions and Thoughts Openly:** Vulnerability fosters intimacy and encourages her to open up as well.
- **Avoiding Distractions When She Is Speaking:** Show that you value her words by giving her your full attention.

Real-Life Examples and Case Studies

Case Study 1: The Power of Empathy

John and Sarah had been dating for six months when Sarah came home upset after a tough day at work. Instead of immediately offering solutions, John simply said, "That sounds like a really difficult day. Tell me more about what happened." This simple act of empathy made Sarah feel heard and supported, strengthening their emotional connection. By practicing empathy, John deepened their bond and built trust, illustrating the power of understanding in relationships.

Case Study 2: Effective Communication in Conflict Resolution

Michael and Rachel often argued about household responsibilities, leading to frustration on both sides. Instead of escalating the conflict, Michael practiced emotional intelligence by acknowledging Rachel's concerns: "I understand that you feel overwhelmed. Let's find a way to divide tasks more fairly." By listening and responding thoughtfully, Michael diffused tension and strengthened their relationship, demonstrating how effective communication can resolve conflicts and enhance connection.

Case Study 3: Recognizing Emotional Cues

David noticed that his girlfriend, Lisa, was unusually quiet during dinner. Instead of ignoring it, he gently asked, "Is something on your mind? You seem a little off today." Lisa then opened up about a stressful situation at work. By recognizing her emotional cues and initiating conversation, David made her feel valued and supported, showcasing the importance of being attuned to a partner's emotional state.

Practical Tips for Understanding Women's Emotions

- **Be Patient:** Emotional understanding takes time and practice; don't rush the process.
- **Stay Curious:** Ask questions to gain deeper insights into her thoughts and feelings, fostering a stronger connection.
- **Avoid Judgment:** Accept her emotions without criticism. Create a safe space where she feels comfortable expressing herself without fear of being judged.
- **Express Appreciation:** Acknowledge and appreciate her emotional depth. Let her know that her feelings are valid and important to you.
- **Learn Her Love Language:** Understanding how she expresses and receives love can significantly strengthen your emotional connection. Whether it's through words of affirmation, acts of service, quality time, gifts, or physical touch, recognizing her love language allows you to connect on a deeper level.

Conclusion

Understanding women's emotions is an essential skill for building meaningful relationships. By recognizing the psychological, biological, and social influences on emotions, developing emotional intelligence, practicing empathy, and applying real-life insights, men can create stronger emotional connections with women. Mastering these skills will not only help in impressing women but also in forming deep, lasting, and fulfilling relationships. As men become more attuned to the emotional landscape of their partners, they pave the way for healthier, more enriching interactions that foster love, trust, and mutual respect. Ultimately, this understanding leads to a more profound appreciation of the complexities of women's emotions, enhancing both personal growth and relational satisfaction.

Chapter 2: Building Confidence and Charisma

Introduction

Confidence and charisma are two of the most attractive qualities a man can possess. They act as powerful magnets that naturally draw people toward you. Women, in particular, are often attracted to men who radiate genuine confidence and charm. However, confidence doesn't mean arrogance, and charisma isn't just about being the loudest person in the room.

In this chapter, you will learn how to develop authentic confidence, enhance your natural charisma, and use these qualities to win the woman of your dreams. The key is to be your best self while making her feel special and appreciated.

The Power of Self-Confidence in Attracting Women

Self-confidence is about believing in yourself and your abilities. It's the assurance you project through your words, actions, and even your body language. When you are confident, you naturally appear more attractive, trustworthy, and appealing to women.

Why Confidence Matters:

- Emotional Stability: Confident men are emotionally stable and don't easily get rattled by rejection or criticism.
- Respect and Admiration: Women respect men who have a strong sense of self-worth.

- Positivity and Optimism: Confidence often goes hand in hand with a positive outlook, which is highly attractive.
- Leadership Qualities: Confident men can take the initiative and make decisions, which many women find appealing.
- Increased Sex Appeal: Confidence directly contributes to a man's perceived attractiveness. Women are instinctively drawn to men who appear comfortable in their own skin and confident in their desires.
- Enhanced Social Skills: Confidence helps you communicate effectively, making conversations more engaging and enjoyable.

Building Unshakeable Confidence

Building unshakeable confidence requires dedication, self-reflection, and continuous growth. Here are essential techniques to establish lasting self-confidence:

Identify and Embrace Your Strengths: Take time to list your strengths, talents, and achievements. Acknowledge what you're good at and celebrate these positive attributes regularly.

Case Study: Rahul was a shy, introverted man who struggled with self-doubt. By making a habit of listing his achievements and embracing his strengths, he gradually built the confidence to approach women and excel in social interactions.

Work on Your Weaknesses: Confidence doesn't mean ignoring your flaws. Identify areas you want to improve and work on them consistently. Self-improvement boosts confidence.

Case Study: Amit had trouble with public speaking, which affected his confidence. After joining a public speaking club and practicing regularly, he not only improved his skill but also gained the confidence to initiate conversations with women effortlessly.

Positive Affirmations: Start your day with positive affirmations. Statements like, "I am confident, capable, and deserving of love" can reprogram your subconscious mind for success.

Step Out of Your Comfort Zone: Challenge yourself to do things that scare you. The more you face your fears, the stronger your confidence becomes.

Case Study: Rajesh was terrified of rejection. He started challenging himself by talking to at least one new person every day. Over time, his confidence grew, and he became much more comfortable approaching women.

Maintain Good Posture: Your body language speaks volumes. Stand tall, make eye contact, and walk with purpose. Good posture projects confidence even when you're feeling nervous.

Practice Mindfulness and Self-Compassion: Learn to be kind to yourself, even when you make mistakes. Mindfulness helps you stay calm and focused, which enhances your overall confidence.

Developing Charisma and Charm

Charisma is often described as a mysterious, magnetic quality that draws people in. But in reality, it's a skill that can be cultivated. Being charismatic doesn't mean being the loudest or most outgoing person in the room—it means being captivating, engaging, and genuinely interested in those around you.

Techniques to Enhance Your Charisma:

Active Listening: Charismatic people make others feel heard and valued. Focus entirely on what she is saying and respond thoughtfully.

Warmth and Approachability: Smile genuinely and maintain a friendly, welcoming demeanor. People are naturally attracted to those who radiate warmth.

Powerful Storytelling: The ability to tell captivating stories can make you more engaging and memorable. Share stories that are humorous, inspiring, or thought-provoking.

Humor and Playfulness: A great sense of humor is one of the most attractive qualities a man can have. Make her laugh, but avoid overdoing it. The key is to be playful and light-hearted.

Being Present: Charismatic people have a strong presence. When you're with her, make her feel like she's the only person that matters. Put away your phone and give her your undivided attention.

Overcoming Insecurities and Boosting Self-Esteem

Insecurity is the enemy of confidence. It's natural to have doubts, but allowing them to control you will only push people away. To overcome insecurity, you must first understand where it stems from.

Common Insecurities Men Face:

- Fear of rejection or failure.
- Comparing yourself to others.
- Physical appearance concerns.
- Feeling unworthy of love or attention.

How to Overcome Insecurity:

Reframe Negative Thoughts: Challenge negative beliefs by replacing them with empowering statements. Instead of thinking, "I'm not good enough," tell yourself, "I am constantly improving and growing."

Stop Comparing Yourself to Others: Your journey is unique. Focus on your own progress rather than measuring yourself against others.

Practice Self-Compassion: Treat yourself with the same kindness you would show a friend. Accept your flaws while working to improve them.

Celebrate Small Wins: Acknowledge your successes, no matter how small. This habit reinforces your sense of achievement and builds confidence.

Grooming and Personal Presentation Tips

Physical appearance is often the first thing women notice, but it's not just about having good looks—it's about presenting yourself well and taking care of your body.

Effective Grooming Tips:

- Maintain good hygiene: Cleanliness is non-negotiable.
- Dress appropriately for the occasion: Wearing well-fitted, clean, and stylish clothes makes a strong impression.
- Haircare: Keep your hair neat and styled.
- Skincare: Take care of your skin to appear fresh and healthy.
- Fitness: Staying in shape not only boosts your confidence but also shows you care about your well-being.

The Difference Between Confidence and Arrogance

It's essential to understand that confidence is not arrogance. Confidence is a quiet assurance in your abilities, whereas arrogance is an exaggerated sense of superiority. Women can easily spot the difference, and arrogance is often a major turn-off.

How to Avoid Appearing Arrogant:

- Be humble and gracious.
- Acknowledge your flaws and be willing to learn.
- Show respect to everyone, regardless of their status or appearance.

Case Study: From Self-Doubt to Self-Assurance

Rahul struggled with self-doubt for years, especially when it came to approaching women. He decided to work on his confidence by setting small, achievable goals, such as starting conversations with strangers and joining a public speaking club. Over time, Rahul's confidence grew, and he became more comfortable in social situations. His newfound self-assurance not only helped him connect with women but also improved his overall quality of life. This example highlights how consistent effort and self-improvement can transform self-doubt into confidence.

Overcoming Self-Doubt and Insecurity

Everyone experiences insecurity at some point. The key is learning how to overcome it and not let it control your actions.

Tips to Overcome Self-Doubt:

1. Challenge Negative Thoughts: Question their validity and replace them with constructive ones. For example, instead of thinking, "I'm not good enough," remind yourself of your achievements.
2. Avoid Comparison: Focus on your journey rather than comparing yourself to others. Everyone has their own path and pace.
3. Acknowledge Your Progress: Celebrate every step forward, no matter how small. Progress, not perfection, is the goal.
4. Surround Yourself with Positivity: Choose people who uplift and inspire you. Positive influences can boost your confidence and motivation.
5. Embrace Failure: Understand that mistakes are part of growth, not proof of inadequacy. Learn from your failures and move forward.

Real-Life Example: Turning Failure into Growth

Amit faced rejection multiple times when asking women out. Instead of letting it discourage him, he used each experience as a learning opportunity. He analyzed what went wrong, worked on his approach, and eventually became more confident in his interactions. His resilience and willingness to learn from failure helped him overcome self-doubt and build lasting confidence.

Projecting Confidence Through Body Language

Your body language speaks louder than words. Projecting confidence physically can enhance your overall appeal.

How to Appear Confident:

1. Maintain Eye Contact: It shows sincerity and interest. Avoid staring, but make sure your gaze is steady and engaging.
2. Stand Tall: Keep your posture upright and relaxed. Slouching can make you appear insecure.
3. Firm Handshake: It reflects strength and self-assurance. A weak handshake can leave a negative impression.
4. Controlled Gestures: Avoid fidgeting or nervous movements. Calm, deliberate gestures convey confidence.
5. Smile Genuinely: A warm smile can instantly make you more approachable. It signals friendliness and positivity.

Case Study: The Charismatic Leader

Arjun was known for his charisma in both his personal and professional life. He had a natural ability to make people feel special and valued. Arjun's secret was his genuine interest in others, his positive attitude, and his ability to communicate with confidence and humor. His charisma not only helped him build strong relationships but also made him a respected leader. This example demonstrates how charisma can enhance your personal and professional life.

Conclusion

Confidence and Charisma are not inherited traits; they are skills you can develop and refine. By enhancing your self-confidence, working on your presentation, and embracing genuine charisma, you will become more attractive and appealing to women. Remember, women are drawn to men who are not only confident but also warm, kind, and engaging.

Chapter 3: Understanding the Body Language

Introduction

Body language serves as a powerful and often unspoken form of communication, conveying emotions and intentions that words may fail to express. When it comes to understanding a woman's feelings toward you, her nonverbal cues can provide invaluable insights. This chapter delves into the intricacies of female body language, equipping you with the tools to discern whether she is genuinely interested in you or subtly signaling her disinterest. By honing your observational skills, you can navigate social interactions with greater confidence and clarity.

Signs of Interest

When a woman is attracted to you, her body language will typically reflect openness, engagement, and enthusiasm. Here are the key indicators to look for:

1. Eye Contact and Pupil Dilation

Prolonged eye contact is one of the most telling signs of interest. If she maintains eye contact with you, it suggests that she is genuinely engaged in the conversation. Additionally, if you notice her pupils dilating while looking at you, this physiological response indicates attraction. Frequent glances followed by shyly looking away can also suggest curiosity and playfulness, signaling that she is intrigued by you.

2. Smiling and Laughter

A genuine smile, characterized by crinkling around the eyes, indicates authentic happiness and interest. If she frequently giggles, especially at your jokes—even the less-than-funny ones—it's a positive sign that she enjoys your company. Furthermore, if she bites her lip or lightly touches her lips while looking at you, it can be a subtle indication of flirtation and attraction.

3. Mirroring Your Actions

Mirroring is a subconscious behavior that occurs when someone feels comfortable and connected with another person. If she subconsciously mimics your gestures, posture, or even speech patterns, it indicates that she is engaged and feels a rapport with you. This mirroring creates a sense of connection and can be a strong indicator of her interest.

4. Leaning In and Body Orientation

Physical proximity and orientation can reveal a lot about her feelings. If she leans in while speaking to you, it shows that she is interested and invested in the conversation. A woman who is attracted to you will typically face you directly, rather than angling her body away. Additionally, if her feet are pointed toward you while seated or standing, it's another sign of subconscious attraction.

5. Playing with Hair and Accessories

When a woman twists or plays with her hair, it often suggests nervous excitement or flirtation. Adjusting her jewelry or clothes while talking to you indicates that she wants to appear more attractive in your eyes. Stroking her neck can also be a subconscious way of drawing attention to her femininity, further signaling her interest.

6. Touching and Physical Proximity

Light, casual touches on your arm or shoulder can signal comfort and interest. If she finds excuses to brush against you or stands close to you, it suggests that she enjoys your presence and is comfortable being near you. Playful nudges or touching your hands during conversation indicate that she is testing your response to her advances, which can be a positive sign.

7. Open Body Language

Open body language is a clear indicator of comfort and receptiveness. Uncrossed arms and a relaxed posture show that she is at ease and open to interaction. If she keeps her palms visible, it signals honesty and openness. Additionally, tilting her head slightly while listening to you indicates deep interest and engagement in what you are saying.

8. Flushed Skin and Blushing

If she blushes while talking to you, it often means she is emotionally engaged and affected by your presence. Flushed skin around her chest or cheeks can be a biological response to attraction, indicating that she is feeling a heightened emotional state in your company.

9. Playfulness and Teasing

Engaging in light-hearted teasing or banter is often a way of expressing attraction. If she playfully challenges you or gives you a nickname, she is likely building a connection and showing that she enjoys your interaction. This playful dynamic can be a strong indicator of her interest.

10. Maintaining Conversations and Asking Personal Questions

If she actively asks about your personal life, hobbies, and future plans, it shows that she is invested in getting to know you better. Women who are interested in a man will often try to extend conversations rather than cut them short, indicating a desire for deeper connection.

Signs of Rejection

Just as positive body language signals interest, certain cues indicate disinterest or discomfort. Recognizing these signs can save you from pursuing someone who isn't reciprocating your feelings.

1. Avoiding Eye Contact or Looking Away Frequently

If she consistently avoids eye contact or looks around the room while talking, it suggests disengagement. Repeatedly checking her phone or appearing distracted during your conversation signals a lack of interest and investment in the interaction.

2. Closed-Off Body Language

Crossing arms or legs can indicate defensiveness or discomfort. If she leans away from you or maintains a significant physical distance, it shows a lack of attraction. Additionally, if she angles her body away from you, she is subconsciously trying to create a barrier between you.

3. Minimal Smiling or Forced Smiles

If her smile appears tight or forced, it may indicate that she is faking politeness rather than genuinely enjoying the conversation. A lack of laughter or forced laughter without enthusiasm suggests that she is not engaged and may be trying to end the interaction.

4. Lack of Physical Contact

If she avoids any form of physical touch, it likely means she does not feel a connection. If she steps back or moves away when you get close, she is clearly setting boundaries and indicating her disinterest.

5. Short or One-Word Responses

If her responses are short, vague, or lack enthusiasm, it may signal that she is not interested in continuing the conversation. If she doesn't ask questions or engage in dialogue, it's a clear sign that she is not invested in the interaction.

6. Fake Excuses to Leave or Cut Conversations Short

If she frequently mentions being busy or needs to leave abruptly, she is likely trying to exit the situation politely. Making excuses for not responding to messages or consistently declining invitations indicates avoidance and disinterest.

7. Lack of Mirroring or Disengagement

If she doesn't match your energy or gestures, it suggests that she isn't invested in the interaction. If she looks bored, frequently checks the time, or shifts in her seat, these behaviors indicate a lack of engagement and interest.

8. Blocking Behaviors

Holding objects between you and her, such as a bag, crossed arms, or even a phone, creates a psychological barrier. If she keeps her hands hidden or clenched, it may indicate that she is feeling uncomfortable or defensive.

9. Absence of Playfulness or Teasing

If she remains formal and does not engage in playful teasing, she likely sees you in a neutral or disinterested way. Avoiding inside jokes or failing to remember details from previous conversations suggests that she doesn't value the connection.

10. Introducing You as a Friend or Mentioning Other Men

If she refers to you as "just a friend," it may indicate that she does not see you romantically. Additionally, if she frequently mentions other men she's interested in, it's a clear sign that she does not view you in a romantic light.

Real-Life Example and Case Study

Case Study: John and Emily

John, a 28-year-old software engineer, met Emily at a social gathering. During their first conversation, he noticed several signs of interest from Emily. She frequently made eye contact, played with her necklace, and leaned in while they spoke. Over time, she began mirroring his gestures and lightly touching his arm during discussions. Recognizing these signs of interest, John confidently asked Emily out, and they soon developed a strong and meaningful connection.

In contrast, John once approached another woman, Lisa, who exhibited clear signs of disinterest. Lisa frequently looked away while talking, crossed her arms, and provided short, unenthusiastic responses. Despite John's efforts to keep the conversation going, Lisa excused herself, stating she was busy. Understanding these nonverbal cues, John realized Lisa was not interested and respectfully moved on, saving himself from further disappointment.

Lesson from the Case Study

This case highlights the importance of accurately reading body language. While Emily's cues indicated attraction and interest, Lisa's signals showed disinterest and discomfort. Being able to differentiate between these signals can help men navigate relationships with confidence and avoid misinterpretations that could lead to awkward situations.

Conclusion

Recognizing a woman's body language can be a game-changer in social and romantic interactions. By understanding the subtle cues of attraction and disinterest, you can significantly improve your chances of building meaningful connections. Pay attention to her nonverbal signals, be respectful of her boundaries, and adjust your approach accordingly. By mastering the art of reading body language, you will navigate relationships with greater confidence and clarity, ultimately leading to more fulfilling interactions.

Chapter- 4: Effective Communication

Introduction:

The Communication is the cornerstone of any successful relationship. It is the bridge that connects two individuals, allowing them to share their thoughts, emotions, and experiences. When it comes to impressing a woman, effective communication is not just about what you say but how you say it. It involves a combination of verbal and non-verbal cues, emotional intelligence, and active listening. Mastering this art can transform your interactions from mundane to meaningful, fostering deeper connections and lasting attraction.

In this chapter, we will explore the importance of communication in building attraction, the key elements of effective communication, and practical strategies to enhance your conversational skills. Through real-life examples and case studies, you will gain insights into how these principles apply in everyday situations, making it easier for you to adopt and implement them.

The Importance of Communication in Attraction

Good communication is not just about talking; it's about connecting. When you communicate effectively, you demonstrate attentiveness, respect, and genuine interest in the other person. This creates a sense of trust and emotional intimacy, which are essential for building attraction and forming meaningful relationships.

Why Communication Matters

1. Building Trust

Trust is the foundation of any relationship. When you communicate openly and honestly, you show that you are reliable and genuine. Consistency in your words and actions reassures the other person that they can depend on you.

Example: If you promise to meet her at a specific time, keeping your word builds trust, while breaking it erodes it.

Case Study: A couple who frequently communicated their needs and expectations openly reported feeling more secure and valued in their relationship. The man's ability to listen attentively and respond thoughtfully to his partner's needs contributed to a healthier bond, ultimately resulting in a long-term relationship.

2. Emotional Connection

Women are often drawn to men who can share their thoughts and feelings openly. When you discuss your dreams, fears, and aspirations, you appear more authentic and relatable. Emotional connection is built when conversations go beyond surface-level topics.

Example: During a date, a man shares his struggles and how he overcame them, sparking admiration and empathy.

Case Study: Aman was initially hesitant to talk about his insecurities with his girlfriend. However, when he finally shared his journey of overcoming anxiety and building his confidence, his girlfriend appreciated his honesty and felt more connected to him.

3. Resolving Misunderstandings

Misunderstandings are inevitable in any relationship. Clear communication helps address issues before they escalate. Being willing to listen to her perspective, acknowledge your mistakes, and clarify misunderstandings are crucial steps.

Example: A married couple who practiced active listening and frequent feedback avoided unnecessary arguments and developed a more peaceful relationship.

Case Study: Aman and Priya often argued about trivial matters. Once they adopted a habit of calmly discussing their issues and actively listening to each other's concerns, their communication improved drastically.

4. Expressing Genuine Interest

By listening attentively and responding thoughtfully, you show that you value her opinions and emotions. This makes her feel appreciated and respected.

Example: A man who remembers little details she shares, such as her favorite book or childhood memory, leaves a positive impression.

Case Study: Suresh met Riya during a weekend getaway. He remembered her passion for wildlife conservation and later shared an article related to her interest, which impressed her and led to them dating.

How to Start a Conversation With a Woman

Approaching a woman can be intimidating, but it doesn't have to be. The key is to approach with confidence and kindness. Starting a conversation effectively is about demonstrating genuine curiosity and being relatable.

Tips for Starting Conversations

1. Observe Your Surroundings

Use your environment to initiate a conversation. This natural approach helps in breaking the ice.

Example: At a party, you could say, "I love the music they're playing. Do you have a favorite song by this artist?"

Case Study: Rahul met Priya at a coffee shop and noticed she was reading a novel by her favorite author. He started the conversation by asking about the book, which led to an engaging discussion and ultimately a strong friendship.

2. Compliment Genuinely

Instead of generic compliments, try something more specific and sincere.

Example: "You have a really charming smile; it's contagious."

Real-Life Example: During a networking event, Ramesh complimented Meera on her confidence during her presentation. She appreciated the observation, leading to a friendly and meaningful conversation.

3. Ask Open-Ended Questions

Questions that require more than a simple "yes" or "no" will keep the conversation flowing.

Example: "What's the most interesting thing you've done this week?"

Tip: This approach encourages her to share more about herself and feel comfortable opening up.

4. Use Humor to Break the Ice

A light-hearted joke or playful comment can instantly put her at ease.

Example: Arjun was waiting in a queue at a bookstore when he joked to a woman nearby, "If this line gets any longer, we might finish reading the entire book before we pay for it." His playful comment led to a fun conversation, and they ended up grabbing coffee afterward.

5. Be Respectful and Authentic

Approach her with genuine interest and respect. Avoid using rehearsed pickup lines, as they often come off as insincere.

Tip: Authenticity is key. Be yourself and let your personality shine through.

The Role of Non-Verbal Communication

Non-verbal cues, such as body language, eye contact, and facial expressions, play a significant role in communication.

They can convey confidence, interest, and empathy, often more effectively than words.

Key Non-Verbal Communication Tips

1. Maintain Eye Contact

Eye contact shows that you are engaged and interested in the conversation.

Tip: Avoid staring, as it can make her uncomfortable. Instead, maintain natural eye contact.

2. Use Open Body Language

Avoid crossing your arms or turning your body away, as this can signal disinterest. Instead, face her directly and lean slightly forward to show attentiveness.

3. Smile Genuinely

A warm smile can make you appear approachable and friendly.

Tip: Ensure your smile is natural and not forced.

4. Pay Attention to Her Non-Verbal Cues

Observe her body language to gauge her comfort level. If she seems relaxed and engaged, continue the conversation. If she appears distracted or uncomfortable, adjust your approach.

Active Listening: The Key to Meaningful Conversations

Active listening involves fully focusing on the speaker, understanding their message, and responding thoughtfully. It shows that you value her thoughts and feelings, fostering a deeper connection.

How to Practice Active Listening

1. Give Her Your Full Attention

Avoid distractions, such as checking your phone or looking around the room.

Tip: Nod occasionally and use verbal affirmations like "I see" or "That's interesting" to show that you're listening.

2. Reflect and Paraphrase

Repeat what she said in your own words to ensure you understood correctly.

Example: "So, you're saying that you enjoy traveling because it allows you to experience new cultures?"

3. Ask Follow-Up Questions

Show genuine curiosity by asking questions related to what she shared.

Example: "What was your favorite destination, and why?"

4. Avoid Interrupting

Let her finish speaking before responding. Interrupting can make her feel unheard or disrespected.

Common Communication Mistakes to Avoid

Even with the best intentions, certain communication habits can hinder your ability to connect with a woman. Being aware of these mistakes can help you avoid them.

Mistakes to Watch Out For

1. Talking Too Much About Yourself

While sharing about yourself is important, dominating the conversation can make her feel unimportant.

Tip: Strike a balance between sharing and listening.

2. Being Overly Critical or Judgmental

Criticizing her opinions or choices can create tension and make her defensive.

Tip: Respect her perspective, even if you disagree.

3. Using Filler Words or Rambling

Excessive use of filler words like "um" or "uh" can make you appear unsure or unprepared.

Tip: Practice speaking clearly and concisely.

4. Ignoring Her Non-Verbal Cues

Failing to notice her body language can lead to misunderstandings.

Tip: Stay attuned to her reactions and adjust your approach accordingly.

Building Emotional Intimacy Through Communication

Emotional intimacy is the foundation of a strong and lasting relationship. It is built through open, honest, and vulnerable communication.

How to Foster Emotional Intimacy

1. Share Your Feelings and Experiences

Open up about your thoughts, emotions, and personal experiences.

Example: Discuss your goals, fears, and what makes you happy.

2. Create a Safe Space for Her to Share

Encourage her to express herself without fear of judgment.

Tip: Be supportive and empathetic when she opens up.

3. Be Vulnerable

Vulnerability is a sign of strength, not weakness. It allows for deeper emotional connections.

Example: Share a personal story about a challenge you faced and how you overcame it.

4. Practice Empathy

Put yourself in her shoes and try to understand her perspective.

Tip: Validate her feelings by saying things like, "I can see why you'd feel that way."

Real-Life Examples and Case Studies

To illustrate the principles discussed in this chapter, let's explore a few real-life examples and case studies.

1. Case Study: Building Trust Through Communication

Karan made a conscious effort to communicate openly with his partner. When they encountered conflicts, instead of shutting down or resorting to arguments, Karan would patiently explain his perspective and listen to hers. This approach strengthened their relationship and minimized misunderstandings.

2. Case Study: Emotional Connection Through Vulnerability

Aman shared his journey of overcoming anxiety with his girlfriend. His honesty and vulnerability made her feel closer to him, deepening their bond.

3. Case Study: Resolving Misunderstandings

Aman and Priya adopted a habit of calmly discussing their issues and actively listening to each other's concerns. This approach enabled them to resolve misunderstandings quickly, enhancing the quality of their relationship.

Conclusion: Effective communication is a skill that can be developed with practice and intention. By being attentive, authentic, and empathetic, you can build trust, foster emotional intimacy, and create lasting connections. Remember, communication is not just about words; it's a holistic experience that transcends mere words, fostering understanding and intimacy in relationships.

Chapter 5: Creating Emotional Attraction and Bonding

Introduction

Physical attraction might get her attention, but emotional attraction is what keeps her interested. When a woman feels emotionally connected to a man, her desire for him deepens beyond mere appearance or superficial charm. Emotional attraction is about creating a genuine bond that makes her feel safe, understood, and appreciated.

In this chapter, we will explore how to build emotional attraction, develop deep connections, and make her feel valued. From emotional intelligence to vulnerability, you'll learn the keys to creating a bond that leaves a lasting impression on her heart. This chapter will cover everything you need to create emotional attraction and bonding through practical advice, psychological insights, and real-life examples.

What Is Emotional Attraction?
Emotional attraction is the connection that goes beyond physical appearance. It's about how someone makes you feel. For women, feeling understood, supported, and appreciated is often more powerful than any physical traits.

Understanding Emotional Attraction from a Psychological Perspective

Psychologically, emotional attraction is rooted in our brain's reward system. When someone makes us feel understood, valued, or emotionally fulfilled, our brain releases dopamine and oxytocin, which strengthen feelings of attachment and affection. Women, in particular, tend to form stronger emotional bonds when these chemicals are activated, which is why emotional attraction plays such a significant role in building deep, lasting connections.

Signs of Emotional Attraction:

1. She enjoys sharing her thoughts and feelings with you.
2. She feels comfortable being herself around you.
3. She shows genuine concern for your well-being.
4. She remembers small details about you.
5. She feels safe and appreciated in your presence.

Case Study: Mark & Priya

Mark was a charming, confident man who easily attracted women. However, his relationships often ended quickly because they were built on superficial attraction. When he met Priya, he decided to focus on creating a deeper connection. He listened to her stories, empathized with her struggles, and celebrated her achievements. By consistently showing emotional support, Mark created a bond with Priya that was much stronger than anything he had experienced before. They are now happily married and credit their success to the emotional foundation they built.

The Power of Emotional Intelligence

Emotional Intelligence (EI) is the ability to understand, manage, and express emotions effectively. It plays a crucial role in building emotional attraction.

Components of Emotional Intelligence:

1. Self-Awareness: Understanding your own emotions and how they influence your behavior.
2. Self-Regulation: Managing your emotions in a healthy, constructive way.
3. Empathy: Understanding and appreciating the emotions of others.
4. Social Skills: Building positive interactions through communication, respect, and sensitivity.
5. Motivation: Pursuing meaningful goals with passion and determination.

How Emotional Intelligence Attracts Women:

- It shows that you can handle life's challenges gracefully.
- It allows you to connect with her on a deeper emotional level.
- It demonstrates your ability to understand and appreciate her feelings.

Real-Life Example: The Emotional Intelligence Difference

A study conducted by Dr. John Gottman revealed that couples with high emotional intelligence have a higher success rate in maintaining long-term relationships. Men who actively listen, validate their partner's feelings, and communicate openly tend to attract women on a much deeper emotional level.

Creating Emotional Connection Through Empathy Empathy is the ability to understand and share someone else's feelings. When you show empathy, you make her feel truly understood and appreciated.

How to Show Empathy:

1. Listen Actively: Pay full attention to her words, emotions, and body language.
2. Acknowledge Her Feelings: Validate her emotions instead of dismissing them.
3. Be Patient and Non-Judgmental: Allow her to express herself without feeling criticized.
4. Ask Thoughtful Questions: Show genuine interest in her experiences and thoughts.
5. Offer Support: Whether it's emotional or practical, be there for her when she needs you.

Case Study: The Empathy Effect

David met Sarah during a difficult phase in her life. Instead of trying to 'fix' her problems, he listened, acknowledged her pain, and provided emotional support without judgment. Sarah found his empathy incredibly attractive and eventually fell in love with him because she felt truly understood.

Building Trust and Safety
Trust is the foundation of any meaningful relationship. Without trust, emotional attraction cannot thrive.

How to Build Trust:

1. Be Reliable: Keep your promises and be consistent in your actions.
2. Be Honest: Share your true thoughts and feelings, even when it's uncomfortable.
3. Respect Boundaries: Respect her personal space and decisions.
4. Admit Your Mistakes: Taking responsibility for your errors shows maturity.

5. Be Supportive: Encourage her dreams and be her cheerleader.

Real-Life Example: Trust Builds Bonds

Sam and Rhea were in a long-distance relationship. Despite the challenges, Sam always made time for her, kept his promises, and showed unwavering support for her ambitions. His reliability and honesty built a strong emotional foundation that led to their successful marriage.

The Art of Vulnerability
Vulnerability is not a weakness; it's a strength that shows authenticity. Sharing your vulnerabilities allows her to see the real you, which helps deepen the emotional connection.

Why Vulnerability Works:

- It shows you are genuine and trustworthy.
- It allows her to feel safe enough to share her own vulnerabilities.
- It creates a deeper, more meaningful bond.

How to Be Vulnerable Without Overdoing It:

1. Share Your Experiences: Talk about your struggles, challenges, and lessons learned.
2. Express Your Emotions: Don't be afraid to show how you feel.
3. Be Open About Your Desires: Share your dreams and aspirations.
4. Balance Vulnerability With Strength: Show resilience even when discussing your weaknesses.

Real-Life Example: Vulnerability Creates Connection

James struggled with expressing his emotions, but when he shared his insecurities and dreams with Maya, she felt closer to him. By being vulnerable, James established a deeper connection that made their relationship thrive.

Effective Communication
Communication is the backbone of any successful relationship. Being able to communicate effectively means more than just talking; it's about listening, understanding, and responding appropriately.

Tips for Effective Communication:

1. **Active Listening:** Focus on what she is saying, avoid interrupting, and respond thoughtfully.
2. **Empathetic Responses:** Show her you understand her feelings by acknowledging them genuinely.
3. **Clarity and Honesty:** Be straightforward and sincere in your words.
4. **Non-Verbal Communication:** Pay attention to body language, eye contact, and tone of voice.
5. **Ask Open-Ended Questions:** Encourage deeper conversations by asking her about her thoughts and feelings.

Real-Life Example: Communication Breakdown

John and Maya had been dating for months, but their relationship felt stagnant. John realized he was mostly talking about himself and rarely asked about her day or her feelings. When he started actively listening and asking meaningful questions, their connection deepened significantly.

Handling Conflicts

Conflicts are inevitable in any relationship. The key is to handle them maturely and constructively.

Conflict Resolution Strategies:

1. **Stay Calm:** Avoid reacting with anger or frustration. Take a deep breath and address the issue calmly.
2. **Focus on the Issue, Not the Person:** Attack the problem, not her character.
3. **Listen to Understand:** Understand her perspective before trying to make her understand yours.
4. **Find Common Ground:** Look for solutions that satisfy both of you.
5. **Apologize and Forgive:** Admit your mistakes and be willing to forgive hers.

Real-Life Example: Conflict Resolution

Alex and Priya often argued over small things. When Alex started using these conflict-resolution strategies, their arguments decreased, and their emotional bond grew stronger.

Consistency

Consistency is what makes her feel secure and valued. It shows that you are reliable, trustworthy, and genuinely interested in building something meaningful.

Why Consistency Matters:

- It builds trust over time.
- It shows your commitment and dedication.
- It helps avoid misunderstandings and confusion.

How to Be Consistent:

1. **Follow Through:** Keep your promises and do what you say you will.
2. **Be Present:** Regularly check in with her emotionally and mentally.
3. **Show Genuine Interest:** Stay engaged and invested in her life.

Real-Life Example: Consistency Pays Off

David and Rhea built their relationship on consistency. Even during busy times, David made sure to check in, listen, and support her. This consistency strengthened their emotional connection, making their relationship thrive.

Chapter 6: Mastering the Art of Romance

Introduction

Romance is the art of making a woman feel cherished, adored, and deeply valued. It's about crafting moments that are magical, heartfelt, and unforgettable. While attraction and emotional connection form the foundation of a relationship, romance is the beautiful structure built upon them. This chapter delves into the nuances of romantic gestures, creative date ideas, and strategies to keep the spark alive throughout your relationship. You'll also discover the secrets of personalized romance that make her feel truly special and unique.

Understanding What Romance Means to Her

Romance is deeply personal and subjective. What feels romantic to one woman may not resonate with another. To truly master the art of romance, you must first understand her unique preferences and desires.

How to Discover Her Romantic Desires:

1. Ask Her Directly: Engage in a casual, non-intrusive conversation about what she finds romantic. For example, ask, "What's the most romantic thing someone has ever done for you?"

2. Observe Her Reactions: Pay attention to how she responds to romantic scenes in movies, songs, or real-life moments.

Does she swoon over grand gestures or prefer subtle, thoughtful acts?

3. Listen to Her Dreams: When she shares her aspirations or fantasies, take note. These insights can guide your romantic efforts.

4. Understand Her Love Language: Identify whether she values words of affirmation, quality time, gifts, acts of service, or physical touch. Tailor your gestures to align with her love language.

Case Study: Anuj and Riya

Anuj often showered Riya with expensive gifts, but she remained unimpressed. After a heartfelt conversation, he discovered that Riya valued quality time over material possessions. By planning meaningful dates and spending uninterrupted time together, Anuj transformed their relationship.

The Power of Thoughtfulness

Romance isn't about grand gestures alone; it's about thoughtfulness and effort. Small, meaningful actions show that you genuinely care and pay attention to her needs and desires.

Small Gestures That Make a Big Difference:

1. Leaving Sweet Notes: A heartfelt note tucked into her purse or on her pillow can brighten her day.

2. Remembering Important Dates: Mark her birthday, anniversaries, and other significant moments in your calendar.

3. Surprising Her with Her Favorite Things: Whether it's her favorite dessert, a book she's been wanting to read, or a playlist of her favorite songs, these gestures show you care.

4. Paying Attention to Her Words: Recall things she mentioned wanting or enjoying and make them happen.

5. Complimenting Her Meaningfully: Instead of generic compliments, focus on her unique qualities, such as her kindness, intelligence, or creativity.

Case Study: Rajeev and Priya

Rajeev noticed Priya admiring a painting at an art gallery. Months later, he surprised her with a replica of that painting on her birthday. The thoughtfulness behind the gesture made it far more special than any expensive gift could.

Creating Romantic Experiences

Romance thrives on shared experiences that evoke joy, intimacy, and excitement. Making memories together strengthens the bond between you.

Ideas for Romantic Experiences:

1. Planning Special Dates: Surprise her with a thoughtfully planned date, whether it's a fancy dinner, a cozy picnic, or an adventurous outing.

2. Writing Love Letters: Pour your heart out in words and share your feelings through a handwritten letter.

3. Cooking Together: Prepare a delicious meal together, enhancing connection and teamwork.

4. Dancing Together: Even if you're not a great dancer, a slow dance at home can be incredibly romantic.

5. Traveling Together: Explore new places, creating beautiful memories along the way.

Case Study: Dev and Simran

Dev surprised Simran with a road trip to her favorite childhood spot. The experience brought them closer and created lasting memories.

Romancing Through Words

Words have immense power. When used effectively, they can touch her heart and soul.

Techniques to Romance Her with Words:

1. Sincere Compliments: Make her feel special by acknowledging her beauty, intelligence, kindness, or creativity.

2. Expressing Gratitude: Tell her how grateful you are to have her in your life.

3. Sharing Dreams and Desires: Let her know your vision for the future and how you see her as a part of it.

4. Writing Poetry or Songs: If you have a creative side, use it to craft something meaningful.

5. Sending Good Morning and Good Night Messages: Small gestures of affection that make her feel valued.

Creating a Romantic Atmosphere

The environment plays a vital role in setting the mood.

Ideas for Creating a Romantic Atmosphere:

1. Candlelit Dinners: Whether at home or at a restaurant, the warm glow of candles adds intimacy.

2. Ambient Music: Choose music that sets a soothing, romantic vibe.

3. Aromatherapy: Light scented candles or use essential oils to enhance the mood.

4. Comfortable Setting: Make her feel comfortable and special.

5. Personal Touches: Add details that show you've put thought into creating the experience.

Case Study: Arjun and Meena

Arjun planned a quiet evening at home with her favorite music, a candlelit dinner, and a heartfelt conversation. Meena felt deeply appreciated and connected.

The Element of Surprise

Surprises add excitement and keep the relationship lively.

How to Surprise Her Effectively:

1. Unexpected Gifts: Give her something she's been wanting but didn't expect you to remember.

2. Spontaneous Outings: Take her on a surprise date or trip.

3. Acts of Kindness: Do something for her without her asking, like preparing her favorite meal.

4. Secret Messages: Leave hidden love notes in places she'll find later.

5. Arranging a Surprise Party: If she loves social gatherings, this can be a delightful gesture.

Keeping the Romance Alive

Sustaining romance over time requires dedication, creativity, and effort.

How to Keep Romance Alive:

1. Continual Effort: Make romance a habit, not just a special occasion.

2. Never Stop Complimenting Her: Genuine compliments always make her feel appreciated.

3. Relive Old Memories: Revisit places you've enjoyed together and talk about special moments.

4. Create New Traditions: Establish meaningful rituals that only the two of you share.

5. Always Show Appreciation: Never take her for granted.

Case Study: Anil and Meera

Anil made it a tradition to write Meera a heartfelt letter every month, reflecting on their relationship and sharing his feelings. This consistent effort kept their romance alive, even after years of marriage.

Handling Rejection Gracefully

Not every romantic gesture will be accepted as you hope. Understanding how to handle rejection is essential.

Tips for Dealing with Rejection:

1. Respect Her Boundaries: If she's not comfortable with a gesture, don't push it.

2. Avoid Taking It Personally: Rejection doesn't mean she doesn't care; it may simply not align with her preferences.

3. Learn and Grow: Use the experience to better understand her needs.

4. Stay Positive: Maintain a positive attitude and focus on what works for both of you.

5. Maintain Dignity: Handle rejection with grace and maturity.

Case Study: Raj and Sneha

Raj planned an elaborate date, but Sneha wasn't comfortable with such grand gestures. Instead of feeling hurt, Raj took her preferences seriously and focused on simpler, thoughtful acts.

Conclusion:

Mastering the art of romance is about consistently showing her that she is valued, admired, and cherished. Romance is not just about impressing her; it's about genuinely making her feel loved and appreciated. By learning her love language, expressing your feelings through words, and showing genuine appreciation, you can create a relationship filled with warmth, connection, and enduring passion.

Chapter 7: Building a Lasting Connection

Introduction

Creating a strong first impression and kindling romance are essential, but the real challenge lies in building a lasting connection. A meaningful and enduring relationship requires emotional depth, compatibility, and continuous effort from both partners. In this chapter, we'll explore how to nurture your bond with her, strengthen emotional intimacy, and build a connection that stands the test of time. We'll delve into the nuances of compatibility, the importance of consistency, and the art of maintaining passion and trust. By the end of this chapter, you'll have a comprehensive understanding of how to create a relationship that is not only romantic but also deeply fulfilling and resilient.

Understanding Compatibility

Compatibility is the harmonious blending of two individuals' personalities, values, beliefs, and lifestyle choices. While differences are natural and can even enrich a relationship, understanding each other's core essence is essential for building a lasting connection. Compatibility isn't about being identical; it's about finding common ground and respecting each other's uniqueness.

Types of Compatibility:

1. Emotional Compatibility: Sharing similar emotional needs, empathy, and emotional support. This means being

able to understand and respond to each other's feelings in a way that feels nurturing and validating.

2. Intellectual Compatibility: Aligning in terms of interests, conversations, and mental stimulation. This involves enjoying discussions, sharing ideas, and challenging each other intellectually.

3. Physical Compatibility: Having mutual attraction and similar preferences in physical intimacy. This includes understanding each other's needs and boundaries in the physical aspect of the relationship.

4. Spiritual Compatibility: Connecting through shared beliefs or mutual respect for different ideologies. This could involve aligning on religious or philosophical views or simply sharing a sense of purpose in life.

5. Lifestyle Compatibility: Finding common ground in daily habits, routines, and future goals. This includes aligning on priorities like career, family, and how you spend your time together.

How to Assess Compatibility:

- Engage in Deep Conversations: Discuss your values, dreams, and fears openly. This will help you understand if your core beliefs align.

- Observe Conflict Resolution: Pay attention to how you handle disagreements. Healthy conflict resolution is a strong indicator of compatibility.

- Notice Shared Enjoyment: Do you genuinely enjoy spending time together, even in mundane activities?

- Assess Mutual Respect: Do you feel respected and understood in the relationship?

- Evaluate Future Goals: Are your long-term aspirations compatible, or can you find a way to support each other's dreams?

Nurturing Emotional Intimacy

Emotional intimacy goes beyond words. It's about feeling deeply understood, accepted, and appreciated by your partner. It's the glue that holds a relationship together during challenging times.

Ways to Build Emotional Intimacy:

1. Open Communication: Encourage honest discussions without judgment. Create a safe space where both of you can express your thoughts and feelings freely.

2. Being Present: Give her your undivided attention during conversations. Put away distractions and truly listen to what she's saying.

3. Sharing Vulnerabilities: Show your true self, flaws and all. Vulnerability fosters trust and deepens emotional connection.

4. Expressing Appreciation: Regularly acknowledge her value in your life. Let her know how much she means to you through words and actions.

5. Offering Emotional Support: Be there for her during challenging times. Whether she's facing a personal struggle or a professional setback, your support can make all the difference.

Case Study: A Tale of True Compatibility

Raj and Priya met during a professional conference. While their personalities were different, they soon realized that their values and life goals aligned. Through open communication and understanding, they built emotional intimacy by sharing personal struggles and dreams. Even when disagreements occurred, they approached conflicts with patience, focusing on solutions rather than blame. Their consistency and effort, combined with mutual respect, allowed them to form a deep and lasting bond. This example illustrates how compatibility and emotional intimacy can transform a budding romance into a meaningful relationship.

The Importance of Consistency and Effort

Consistency is the backbone of any long-term connection. It proves your commitment and builds trust over time. Relationships thrive when both partners consistently show up for each other, even in small ways.

How to Maintain Consistency:

1. Keep Your Promises: Never make promises you can't keep. Follow through on your commitments, no matter how small.

2. Regular Check-Ins: Ask her how she's feeling and if there's anything you can do better. This shows that you care about her well-being.

3. Express Love Regularly: Through words, gestures, and actions. Don't assume she knows how you feel—show her.

4. Be Reliable: Make her feel secure by being dependable and steady. Consistency in your actions builds trust.

5. Continually Grow Together: Never stop working on the relationship. Attend workshops, read books, or seek counseling if needed to strengthen your bond.

Building Trust and Security

Trust is the foundation of lasting love. Without it, even the strongest attraction will eventually crumble. Trust is built through honesty, reliability, and mutual respect.

How to Build and Maintain Trust:

1. Honesty and Transparency: Share your thoughts and intentions openly. Avoid keeping secrets or hiding important information.

2. Reliability: Be dependable in your actions and words. If you say you'll do something, follow through.

3. Respecting Her Privacy: Allow her the space to be herself. Trust her to make her own decisions and respect her boundaries.

4. Being Supportive: Encourage her personal growth and dreams. Celebrate her successes and stand by her during challenges.

5. Owning Your Mistakes: Apologize sincerely when you're wrong. Taking responsibility for your actions shows maturity and builds trust.

Effective Conflict Resolution

Every relationship faces conflicts, but how you handle them determines the strength of your bond. Healthy conflict resolution involves patience, understanding, and a willingness to compromise.

Steps to Resolve Conflicts Gracefully:

1. Stay Calm and Patient: Avoid reacting out of anger. Take a moment to collect your thoughts before responding.

2. Listen Actively: Understand her point of view before responding. Show empathy and validate her feelings.

3. Use "I" Statements: Focus on expressing your feelings without blaming. For example, say, "I feel hurt when…" instead of "You always…"

4. Seek Compromise: Find solutions that work for both of you. Relationships are about teamwork, not winning arguments.

5. Forgive and Move On: Let go of grudges to maintain harmony. Holding onto past conflicts can erode trust and intimacy.

The Art of Reassurance and Comfort

In a lasting relationship, reassurance and comfort are essential for emotional security. They help her feel valued, loved, and supported.

How to Provide Reassurance:

1. Express Your Feelings: Regularly remind her how much she means to you. Use words, gestures, and actions to show your love.

2. Be Supportive During Tough Times: Offer a listening ear and emotional comfort. Sometimes, just being there is enough.

3. Avoid Taking Her for Granted: Never assume she knows how you feel—show her. Small acts of kindness can go a long way.

4. Physical Touch: Sometimes, a simple hug can communicate more than words. Physical affection fosters emotional closeness.

5. Celebrating Her Successes: Show enthusiasm and pride in her achievements. Be her biggest cheerleader.

Maintaining Passion and Attraction

Passion isn't something you find; it's something you nurture. Keeping the spark alive is essential for a long-lasting connection.

Ways to Maintain Passion:

1. Surprise Her Regularly: Whether it's a romantic date or a thoughtful gesture, keep things exciting.

2. Continual Flirting: Never stop complimenting her and showing attraction. Keep the playful energy alive.

3. Trying New Experiences Together: Bonding through fresh activities can keep the relationship dynamic. Explore hobbies, travel, or take classes together.

4. Prioritizing Physical Intimacy: Make sure your emotional and physical connection remain strong. Communicate openly about your needs and desires.

5. Supporting Her Growth: Encourage her to pursue her dreams and aspirations. A relationship thrives when both partners feel fulfilled individually.

Real-Life Example: Nurturing Passion Through New Experiences

A couple, Rohan and Meera, after several years of marriage, felt their relationship growing stagnant. Instead of letting things fall apart, they decided to explore new activities together. From cooking classes to travel adventures, they rekindled their passion by continually creating shared memories. Their efforts demonstrated how keeping things fresh can preserve passion and strengthen their connection.

Conclusion:

Building a lasting connection requires effort, patience, and dedication. It's not about achieving perfection but rather creating something meaningful and enduring. When you continuously work on nurturing emotional intimacy, trust, and compatibility, your bond will grow stronger with time. Remember, a successful relationship is a journey, not a destination. By prioritizing each other's needs, communicating openly, and maintaining consistency, you can create a love that stands the test of time.

Chapter 8: Communicating Effectively and Resolving Misunderstandings

Introduction

Communication is the lifeline of every successful relationship. It's not only about talking but also about listening, understanding, and responding with compassion. Misunderstandings are inevitable, but with effective communication, they can be resolved gracefully. This chapter will delve into mastering the art of communication, avoiding common pitfalls, and turning conflicts into opportunities for growth. By the end of this chapter, you'll have a deeper understanding of how to communicate effectively, adapt to her communication style, and resolve misunderstandings in a way that strengthens your bond.

The Fundamentals of Effective Communication

Effective communication goes beyond words. It encompasses tone, body language, intent, and timing. When done right, it fosters trust, understanding, and emotional intimacy.

Key Elements of Communication:

1. Clarity: Being straightforward with your thoughts and feelings is crucial. When you express yourself clearly, she feels understood, which fosters trust. For example, instead of saying, "You always ignore me," you could say, "I feel hurt when I don't feel heard." Clarity eliminates ambiguity and ensures your message is received as intended.

2. Active Listening: Focus entirely on what she's saying without interruption. Active listening involves being present, acknowledging her words, and making her feel valued. Example: When she is sharing her concerns, maintain eye contact and respond with statements like, "I understand why you feel that way."

3. Empathy: Understanding her perspective and validating her emotions is essential. Empathy is not just about agreeing but truly grasping how she feels and why. Example: "I can see that you're upset because I wasn't there for you when you needed support." Empathy builds emotional connection and shows that you care.

4. Non-Verbal Cues: Maintaining eye contact, being mindful of your facial expressions and gestures, and having a calm tone of voice can greatly influence how your message is received. Non-verbal communication often speaks louder than words.

5. Respect and Kindness: Approaching every conversation with a kind, non-judgmental attitude shows that you care about her feelings and opinions. This helps in building a solid foundation of trust.

The Art of Active Listening

Active listening is about genuinely hearing and understanding what she's communicating, not just waiting for your turn to speak. It's a skill that requires patience, empathy, and attention.

How to Practice Active Listening:

1. Give Full Attention: Put away distractions like your phone or television and focus entirely on her. This shows that you value her and the conversation.

2. Acknowledge Her Feelings: Nodding, smiling, and responding with phrases like, “I understand,” or “I see,” can make her feel valued.

3. Avoid Interrupting: Let her finish her thoughts before you respond. Interruptions can be perceived as dismissive.

4. Reflect and Clarify: Paraphrasing what she said to ensure understanding is a powerful tool. For instance, “So, you’re feeling frustrated because you think I don’t listen?”

5. Ask Open-Ended Questions: Encourage her to elaborate by asking, “How did that make you feel?” or “What do you think about it?”

Case Study: The Power of Active Listening

Rahul and Ananya were struggling with frequent arguments. Rahul realized that he often interrupted Ananya during conversations, making her feel unheard. He decided to practice active listening by giving her his full attention, acknowledging her feelings, and avoiding interruptions. Over time, Ananya felt more valued, and their arguments decreased significantly. This example highlights how active listening can transform communication and strengthen a relationship.

Expressing Your Feelings Effectively

Being able to communicate your thoughts and emotions clearly is essential for a healthy connection. Expressing feelings effectively requires courage, honesty, and careful phrasing.

Tips for Effective Expression:

1. Use "I" Statements: Instead of accusing her, focus on how her actions make you feel. Example: "I feel hurt when I'm not heard."

2. Be Honest, But Gentle: Share your feelings without sounding accusatory or harsh. Example: "I felt disappointed when we couldn't spend time together."

3. Timing Matters: Choose the right time and place for sensitive discussions. For instance, avoid discussing serious issues when either of you is stressed or distracted.

4. Stay Focused: Avoid bringing up past issues unless relevant to the current discussion. Refrain from saying, "You always do this."

5. Be Solution-Oriented: Always aim for a resolution rather than just venting. Suggesting possible solutions shows your willingness to improve the relationship.

Understanding Her Communication Style

Everyone communicates differently. Understanding her style is crucial to building rapport and harmony.

Different Communication Styles:

1. Direct Communicators: Prefer clear, straightforward conversations. Respond well to honesty and directness.

2. Indirect Communicators: May hint or imply their feelings rather than stating them outright. Gentle probing helps them open up.

3. Emotional Communicators: Express feelings passionately and openly. They value empathy and validation.

4. Rational Communicators: Focus on facts and logical reasoning. Appreciating their logic and addressing their concerns effectively strengthens the relationship.

How to Adapt to Her Style:

- Notice her preference and adjust your approach accordingly.

- If she's indirect, learn to pick up on subtle hints.

- If she's emotional, be empathetic and patient.

- If she's rational, present your points logically and factually.

Handling Misunderstandings Gracefully

Misunderstandings happen, but how you address them determines the health of your relationship.

Steps to Resolve Misunderstandings:

1. Acknowledge the Issue: Admit when something is wrong and address it.

2. Stay Calm and Composed: Avoid reacting emotionally.

3. Listen First, Speak Later: Hear her side fully before presenting yours.

4. Apologize When Necessary: If you're wrong, own up to it without hesitation.

5. Find Common Ground: Seek solutions that benefit both parties.

Real-Life Example: Resolving a Misunderstanding

Priya and Arjun had a misunderstanding when Arjun forgot their anniversary. Instead of getting angry, Priya calmly expressed her feelings, saying, "I felt hurt when you forgot our special day." Arjun listened, apologized sincerely, and planned a surprise dinner to make up for it. This approach not only resolved the issue but also strengthened their bond.

Turning Conflicts into Growth Opportunities

Every conflict holds the potential for deeper understanding and growth. Evaluating disagreements can help you build a stronger relationship.

How to Grow from Conflicts:

1. Reflect and Learn: Analyze what could be improved.

2. Adjust Your Approach: Make changes based on past experiences.

3. Strengthen Trust: Each resolved conflict makes your bond stronger.

4. Express Gratitude: Acknowledge her patience and effort.

5. Celebrate Reconciliation: Enjoy positive moments together after resolving conflicts.

The Power of Apologizing and Forgiving

Acknowledging mistakes and offering sincere apologies go a long way. Forgiveness fosters healing, rebuilding trust, and strengthening emotional bonds. A simple apology followed by consistent efforts to improve your behavior shows genuine commitment.

How to Apologize Effectively:

1. Be Sincere: Mean what you say.

2. Take Responsibility: Acknowledge your mistake without making excuses.

3. Express Regret: Show that you understand the impact of your actions.

4. Make Amends: Offer to fix the situation or prevent it from happening again.

5. Follow Through: Show consistent effort to improve.

Maintaining Healthy Communication Over Time

Consistency is key. Regularly check in on your relationship's communication health. Adjusting to each other's evolving needs and being open to feedback ensures that communication remains effective.

Tips for Maintaining Healthy Communication:

1. Regular Check-Ins: Ask her how she's feeling and if there's anything you can do better.

2. Be Open to Feedback: Accept constructive criticism without defensiveness.

3. Adapt to Changes: As your relationship evolves, so should your communication style.

4. Celebrate Milestones: Acknowledge and celebrate your progress together.

5. Prioritize Quality Time: Spend uninterrupted time together to strengthen your connection.

Case Study: The Journey of Consistent Communication

Suresh and Meera had been married for ten years. Over time, they noticed their communication had become routine and less meaningful. They decided to prioritize regular check-ins, open feedback, and quality time. By making these changes, they rekindled their emotional connection and strengthened their bond. This example illustrates the importance of consistent effort in maintaining healthy communication.

Conclusion:

Effective communication is the cornerstone of a successful relationship. By mastering active listening, expressing your feelings clearly, and resolving misunderstandings gracefully, you can build a deep and lasting connection. Remember, communication is a continuous process that requires effort, patience, and adaptability. When you prioritize understanding and empathy, you create a relationship that thrives on trust, respect, and love.

Chapter 9: Cultivating Emotional and Physical Intimacy

Introduction

While emotional intimacy builds a strong foundation of trust and connection, physical intimacy deepens that bond through affection, passion, and shared experiences. Both aspects are essential for a fulfilling relationship, but they require understanding, sensitivity, and effort. Emotional intimacy allows you to feel safe, understood, and appreciated, while physical intimacy fosters closeness and passion. Together, they create a harmonious balance that strengthens your relationship. In this chapter, we'll explore how to nurture emotional and physical intimacy, strike a healthy balance, and create an environment of lasting romance. By the end of this chapter, you'll have a deeper understanding of how to cultivate both forms of intimacy and maintain a relationship that is both emotionally and physically fulfilling.

Understanding Emotional Intimacy

Emotional intimacy is the glue that holds relationships together. It's about feeling safe, understood, and appreciated by your partner. It goes beyond mere words and actions; it's the emotional resonance and sense of belonging you feel when you are deeply connected to someone. Many people confuse emotional intimacy with romantic gestures, but it's much more about the comfort of being your true self without fear of judgment. Emotional intimacy is built through consistent effort, open communication, and mutual respect.

Signs of Emotional Intimacy:

1. Open Communication: Both of you can share your thoughts and feelings freely. This means being able to express your innermost thoughts and emotions without hesitation. It involves not only talking about your day but also discussing your dreams, fears, and aspirations. Open communication creates a safe space where both partners feel heard and valued.

2. Trust and Safety: Feeling secure enough to be vulnerable. Trust doesn't develop overnight; it's built gradually through consistent honesty and reliability. Trust also means believing in her intentions and having confidence in the strength of your relationship. When trust is present, both partners feel safe to share their deepest fears and insecurities without fear of judgment.

3. Empathy and Understanding: Making an effort to truly understand her emotions. Being empathetic means trying to feel what she feels. It involves acknowledging her perspective even if you don't agree with it. Empathy fosters a deeper connection and shows that you genuinely care about her well-being.

4. Emotional Support: Offering comfort and encouragement during tough times. Emotional support is about being there for her during her lows and cheering for her successes. It's about

being her rock when she needs you and celebrating her achievements as if they were your own.

5. Shared Goals and Dreams: Working together toward a common future. Couples who plan and dream together are more likely to stay emotionally connected. Shared goals create a sense of unity and purpose, strengthening the bond between partners.

Case Study: James and Priya

James and Priya had been dating for a few months when Priya realized that James was unwilling to discuss his feelings about his stressful job. After gently encouraging him to open up and actively listening without interrupting, Priya created a safe space for James to be vulnerable. This openness strengthened their bond significantly. James felt understood and supported, while Priya felt closer to him emotionally. This example highlights the importance of open communication and empathy in building emotional intimacy.

Real-Life Example: Sam and Aisha

Sam and Aisha had been married for ten years. Despite facing financial troubles, their relationship remained strong because they could rely on each other emotionally. Aisha's trust in Sam's ability to provide emotional support made her feel safe even during challenging times. Sam, in turn, felt valued and appreciated for his efforts. Their ability to communicate openly and support each other emotionally helped them navigate difficult situations together. This example demonstrates how trust and emotional support can sustain a relationship through tough times.

Nurturing Emotional Intimacy

Building emotional intimacy requires consistent effort and intentional actions. Here are some ways to nurture emotional intimacy in your relationship:

1. Practice Active Listening: Give her your full attention when she speaks. Avoid interrupting and show genuine interest in what she's saying.

2. Be Vulnerable: Share your own thoughts and feelings openly. Vulnerability fosters trust and encourages her to do the same.

3. Show Empathy: Try to understand her perspective and validate her emotions. Even if you don't agree, acknowledging her feelings shows that you care.

4. Express Appreciation: Regularly acknowledge her efforts and contributions to the relationship. Small gestures of gratitude can go a long way in strengthening emotional intimacy.

5. Spend Quality Time Together: Engage in activities that allow you to connect on a deeper level. Whether it's a heartfelt conversation or a shared hobby, quality time strengthens your bond.

The Role of Physical Intimacy

Physical intimacy is an essential component of a healthy relationship. It's not just about physical attraction; it's about expressing love, affection, and passion. Physical intimacy includes everything from holding hands and cuddling to more intimate moments. It's a way to connect on a deeper level and show your partner that you care.

How to Nurture Physical Intimacy:

1. Communicate Your Needs: Talk openly about your desires and boundaries. Clear communication ensures that both partners feel comfortable and respected.

2. Be Affectionate: Small gestures like holding hands, hugging, or kissing can strengthen your connection.

3. Prioritize Intimacy: Make time for physical intimacy, even in the midst of a busy schedule. It's an important way to maintain closeness.

4. Be Attentive: Pay attention to her needs and preferences. Physical intimacy is about mutual satisfaction and connection.

5. Keep the Spark Alive: Surprise her with romantic gestures or spontaneous acts of affection. Keeping things exciting helps maintain passion in the relationship.

Striking a Healthy Balance

Emotional and physical intimacy are interconnected. A healthy relationship requires a balance of both. Here's how to strike that balance:

1. Prioritize Emotional Connection: Emotional intimacy lays the foundation for physical intimacy. Focus on building trust and understanding first.

2. Communicate Openly: Discuss your needs and expectations for both emotional and physical intimacy.

3. Be Patient: Building intimacy takes time. Be patient and allow your relationship to grow naturally.

4. Be Consistent: Make an effort to nurture both forms of intimacy regularly. Consistency is key to maintaining a strong connection.

5. Celebrate Your Bond: Acknowledge and appreciate the intimacy you share. Celebrate your connection and the love you've built together.

Conclusion:

Emotional and physical intimacy are the cornerstones of a fulfilling relationship. By nurturing both, you create a bond that is deep, meaningful, and lasting. Emotional intimacy fosters trust and understanding, while physical intimacy strengthens your connection through affection and passion. Together, they create a harmonious balance that keeps your relationship strong and vibrant. Remember, intimacy is not a one-time effort but a continuous journey. By prioritizing open communication, empathy, and mutual respect, you can build a relationship that thrives on both emotional and physical intimacy.

Chapter 10: Manipulating Women's Feelings with Dark Psychology Tricks

Introduction

Dark psychology delves into the psychological tactics employed to control or influence others, particularly in interpersonal relationships. These manipulative techniques can evoke strong emotional reactions, fostering dependency and attachment. While they may yield immediate results, the long-term repercussions can be profoundly damaging. This chapter examines key psychological manipulation methods, including Love Bombing, Negging, and emotional push-pull dynamics, supported by real-life case studies to illustrate their effects, pros and cons, and the timing and duration of their impact.

Key Manipulation Techniques

1. Providing Attention and Suddenly Ignoring

One of the most effective psychological tricks is the intermittent reinforcement of attention. By alternating between showering a woman with affection and then abruptly withdrawing it, a manipulator creates emotional confusion, compelling her to crave validation and pursue the attention she once received.

Case Study: Rahul and Simran

Rahul met Simran at a social event and quickly became her ideal companion. He texted her daily, showered her with compliments, and made her feel uniquely special. However, just as Simran began to feel emotionally invested, Rahul withdrew—ignoring her texts, canceling plans, and acting distant. This sudden change triggered anxiety in Simran, leading her to chase after Rahul's affection, desperate to regain what she had lost.

Psychological Effect

This push-and-pull tactic exploits a person's fear of loss and their inherent need for validation. The unpredictability of attention creates an addictive emotional response, making the target increasingly dependent on the manipulator.

Pros and Cons

Pros: Can create a strong emotional bond and keep the target engaged.

Cons: Leads to anxiety, insecurity, and potential emotional trauma.

Duration and Timing

The effects can vary; initial attention may last weeks, while withdrawal can create prolonged emotional distress, often lasting months or longer.

2. Love Bombing: Overwhelming with Affection

Love Bombing is an intense form of emotional manipulation where an individual inundates their target with excessive love, compliments, and affection to forge a rapid emotional attachment. Once the target is emotionally invested, the manipulator may alter their behavior to exert control or withdraw affection.

Case Study: Aman and Riya

Aman met Riya on a dating app and quickly began sending her long, romantic messages, making grand gestures, and constantly reassuring her of his deep feelings. Riya, overwhelmed by this affection, reciprocated swiftly. However, once Aman felt he had secured control over her emotions, he began to withdraw, becoming critical and distant. Riya, confused by this sudden shift, tried harder to regain the love she initially received.

Psychological Effect

Love Bombing fosters a powerful emotional dependency. The recipient becomes addicted to the overwhelming affection and strives to maintain it, even when the manipulator begins to exhibit negative behaviors.

Pros and Cons

Pros: Quickly establishes a strong emotional connection and can make the target feel valued.

Cons: Can lead to emotional dependency and confusion when affection is withdrawn.

Duration and Timing

The initial phase of Love Bombing can last from a few days to several weeks, while the subsequent withdrawal can create lasting emotional scars that may take months to heal.

3. Negging: Undermining Self-Esteem

Negging is a psychological tactic that employs subtle insults

or backhanded compliments to lower a woman’s self-esteem, prompting her to seek validation from the manipulator.

Case Study: Varun and Megha

Varun was charming but often made comments like, “You’re cute, but I bet you don’t get approached much,” or “You have an interesting style—it’s different.” Initially confident, Megha began to doubt herself and sought Varun’s approval more, gradually becoming more emotionally invested in him.

Psychological Effect

Negging instills insecurity, compelling the target to prove their worth. The manipulator becomes a source of validation, enhancing their control over the target’s emotions.

Pros and Cons

Pros: Can create a sense of dependency and increase the manipulator's perceived value.

Cons: Leads to long-term self-esteem issues and emotional distress for the target.

Duration and Timing

The effects of negging can accumulate over time, often manifesting as chronic insecurity that can last indefinitely, depending on the target's resilience and support system.

4. Emotional Push-Pull Dynamics

Emotional unpredictability, such as oscillating between affection and sudden anger, creates instability that keeps the target emotionally engaged, as they strive to avoid displeasing the manipulator.

Case Study: Karan and Sneha

Karan frequently praised Sneha, calling her the most amazing woman he had ever met. Yet, at random moments, he would become irritated, accusing her of being distant or unappreciative. This emotional volatility made Sneha anxious, driving her to please Karan and avoid his anger.

Psychological Effect

Such unpredictability can lead to trauma bonding, where the target becomes reliant on moments of affection and works harder to prevent anger, deepening their attachment to the manipulator.

Pros and Cons

Pros: Keeps the target engaged and eager to please, reinforcing the manipulator's control.

Cons: Creates emotional instability and can lead to significant psychological trauma.

Duration and Timing

The push-pull dynamic can create a cycle of emotional highs and lows that may last for months or even years, depending on the manipulator's behavior and the target's willingness to endure the emotional turmoil.

Conclusion

Dark psychology techniques such as Love Bombing, Negging, and emotional push-pull dynamics can forge intense emotional attachments but often culminate in toxic relationships. Understanding these tactics is crucial for individuals to recognize manipulation and avoid emotional dependency. While these methods may seem effective for gaining attention, they are ultimately harmful and should be replaced with authentic emotional connections grounded in mutual respect and understanding. Recognizing the signs of manipulation can empower individuals to foster healthier, more fulfilling relationships.

Chapter 11: Navigating Rejection Gracefully

Introduction

Rejection is an unavoidable aspect of life, particularly in the realm of romantic pursuits. It is an old Saying: Rejection is more painful then selection. While it can be painful and disheartening, mastering the art of handling rejection with grace is essential for maintaining confidence, emotional equilibrium, and self-respect. Rather than perceiving rejection as a failure, it should be embraced as a valuable opportunity for personal growth, self-improvement, and the development of resilience.

Respect Her Boundaries

One of the most critical components of gracefully managing rejection is the ability to respect a woman's boundaries. Each individual possesses their own comfort zones and preferences, and it is vital to recognize and honor these limits.

Case Study: Rahul and Priya

Rahul had harbored feelings for Priya for several months. One evening, he mustered the courage to express his emotions by asking her out on a date. Priya, while appreciative of his honesty and bravery, gently informed him that she did not envision their relationship evolving beyond friendship. Although Rahul felt a wave of disappointment wash over him, he chose to respect her decision. Instead of insisting on his feelings or becoming upset, he maintained their friendship with maturity and grace. Over time, Priya came to admire his emotional intelligence, and their bond remained strong and intact.

Lesson Learned

Respecting her boundaries is a clear indication of emotional intelligence and self-respect. Pushing too hard or attempting to manipulate the situation can lead to discomfort and potentially damage any existing relationship. Women tend to appreciate men who honor their decisions without resorting to guilt or pressure.

Avoid Taking It Personally

It is crucial to understand that rejection does not define your worth as an individual. A woman's choice not to reciprocate your feelings may stem from her personal preferences, current life circumstances, or emotional state, rather than any inherent flaw in you.

Case Study: Arjun and Neha

After a few pleasant interactions, Arjun decided to ask Neha out. She politely declined, explaining that she was not in a place to pursue a relationship at that moment. Initially, Arjun felt a sense of inadequacy, questioning his attractiveness and personality. However, after taking some time to reflect, he came to the realization that Neha's decision was not a critique of him but rather a personal choice based on her current situation.

Lesson Learned

When you faced rejection, it is essential to avoid internalizing it as a personal failure. Instead, recognize that chemistry and timing play significant roles in relationships. Understanding this perspective will help you maintain your self-confidence and encourage you to keep moving forward in your romantic endeavors.

Learn and Grow

Every rejection presents an opportunity to gain valuable insights into what works and what doesn't in the realm of dating and relationships. Rather than dwelling on disappointment, take the time to analyze the situation and learn from it to improve your approach in the future.

Case Study: Rohit's Dating Journey

Rohit found himself frequently being friend-zoned in his dating life. Instead of placing blame on the women he encountered, he decided to take a step back and analyze his interactions. He realized that he often avoided direct communication about his feelings, which led to ambiguity in his relationships. After working on his confidence and learning to express himself more openly, he began to see better results in his future interactions.

Lesson Learned

Reflecting on past experiences is a crucial step in personal development. Identifying areas for improvement—whether in communication, presentation, or understanding women's perspectives—can significantly enhance your future interactions and relationships.

Stay Positive

Maintaining a positive mindset is essential to ensure that rejection does not become an insurmountable obstacle but rather a stepping stone toward finding the right partner. Confidence and optimism are attractive qualities that can help you overcome setbacks and continue your journey.

Case Study: Kunal's Optimism

Kunal faced multiple rejections while searching for a serious relationship. Instead of allowing bitterness to take root, he chose to remain optimistic, continued to socialize, and focused on his personal growth. Eventually, he met someone who genuinely appreciated his qualities, demonstrating that persistence and a positive attitude can lead to success.

Lesson Learned

A positive attitude not only makes you more appealing but also helps you navigate the complexities of dating. Women are often drawn to men who exude confidence, composure, and resilience, even in the face of setbacks. The ability to maintain confidence in oneself, despite experiencing rejection, is a powerful and attractive trait.

Maintain Dignity

How you respond to rejection speaks volumes about your character and emotional maturity. Handling rejection with grace and dignity preserves your self-respect and leaves a lasting impression on others.

Case Study: Ankit's Maturity

Ankit decided to confess his feelings to his colleague, Riya. When she politely turned him down, he expressed gratitude for her honesty and continued to treat her with respect in their professional environment. Riya admired his maturity and composure, and later introduced him to a friend who turned out to be a great match for him.

Lesson Learned

Lashing out, displaying resentment, or begging for another chance can severely damage your image and reputation. Maintaining composure and dignity in the face of rejection ensures that you leave the situation with your self-respect intact and may even open new doors for future opportunities.

How to Handle Rejection

Effectively handling rejection is not merely about avoiding negativity; it is about responding in a manner that enhances your personal growth and future interactions. Here are some strategies to handle rejection effectively:

1. Acknowledge Your Feelings: It is entirely normal to feel disappointed or hurt. Accept your emotions rather than suppressing them, as this is a crucial step in the healing process.

2. Don't Overanalyze: Avoid obsessing over what went wrong or what you could have done differently. Not all rejections have a deep-rooted reason; sometimes, it simply comes down to a lack of compatibility.

3. Maintain Self-Worth: Remind yourself of your strengths and unique qualities. Do not allow rejection to define your value as a person.

4. Engage in Self-Improvement: Use the experience as a catalyst for personal growth. Work on areas that may need improvement, such as communication skills or emotional intelligence.

5. Move Forward Gracefully: Resist the urge to dwell on rejection. Keep socializing and exploring new opportunities without harboring bitterness or resentment.

6. Seek Support if Needed: If you find it challenging to process your emotions, consider talking to a trusted friend or mentor who can provide perspective and guidance.

Conclusion:

Rejection is an inherent part of life, but how you choose to handle it ultimately determines your personal growth and future success in relationships. By respecting her boundaries, avoiding personalizing the experience, learning from past encounters, maintaining a positive outlook, and preserving your dignity, you can transform setbacks into valuable lessons. Women appreciate men who exhibit emotional maturity, confidence, and resilience, making these qualities essential for achieving long-term romantic success. Embracing rejection as a stepping stone rather than a stumbling block will empower you to navigate the complexities of love and relationships with grace and poise.

Chapter 12: Becoming the Man She Can't Resist

Introduction

Becoming irresistible to women isn't just about charm or good looks—it's about continuous self-improvement and personal growth. Women are naturally drawn to men who are constantly striving to better themselves, not just for the sake of impressing others but for their own fulfillment. Personal growth is the cornerstone of maintaining your appeal and creating a lasting impression. It's about evolving into the best version of yourself, both for your own benefit and for the benefit of your relationship. This chapter will guide you on how to enhance your personal growth effectively, maintain her interest over time, and become the man she can't resist. By the end of this chapter, you'll have a clear roadmap to self-improvement, relationship maintenance, and becoming a man who is not only attractive but also deeply respected and valued.

Constant Self-Improvement: The Key to Irresistibility

Constant self-improvement is the cornerstone of maintaining your appeal. Women are attracted to men who are continuously striving to better themselves in every aspect of life. Personal growth isn't just about achieving external success; it's about developing your character, skills, and emotional intelligence. It's about becoming a well-rounded individual who is confident, passionate, and kind.

Ways to Improve Yourself:

1. Expand Your Knowledge: Never stop learning. Whether it's related to your career, personal interests, or even her interests, knowledge enhances your conversation skills and demonstrates your drive to grow. Reading books, attending workshops, or taking online courses are great ways to expand your knowledge.

2. Enhance Your Skills: Whether it's cooking, dancing, or playing an instrument, learning new skills adds versatility to your personality. It shows that you're willing to step out of your comfort zone and try new things.

3. Maintain Physical Fitness: Staying in shape and maintaining good health is not only attractive but also a sign of discipline and dedication. Regular exercise and a healthy lifestyle boost your confidence and energy levels.

4. Develop Emotional Intelligence: Improving empathy, social skills, and communication abilities makes you more understanding and supportive, which is highly attractive to women. Emotional intelligence helps you navigate relationships with grace and compassion.

5. Stay Passionate About Life: Pursue your dreams with enthusiasm and drive. Passionate men are often the most inspiring. Whether it's your career, a hobby, or a personal goal, your passion will make you more attractive and engaging.

Case Study: Rohit's Journey of Self-Improvement

Rohit, a software engineer, began learning about psychology and emotional intelligence. His newfound knowledge made him more understanding and compassionate, which greatly enhanced his relationship with Priya. Rohit's commitment to personal growth not only improved his relationship but also made him a more confident and fulfilled individual. This example highlights how expanding your knowledge and developing emotional intelligence can transform your relationships and personal life.

Real-Life Example: Aman's Creative Pursuit

Aman, who never considered himself creative, decided to take up photography. His newfound passion not only impressed his girlfriend but also made him more confident and expressive. Aman's willingness to explore a new hobby added depth to his personality and brought a new dimension to his relationship. This example demonstrates how learning new skills can enhance your appeal and create shared interests.

Case Study: Karan's Fitness Journey

Karan's consistent workout routine inspired his girlfriend to start a fitness journey of her own. This shared activity brought them closer and created a sense of teamwork and mutual support. Karan's dedication to physical fitness not only improved his health but also strengthened his relationship. This example illustrates how maintaining physical fitness can have a positive impact on both your personal life and your relationship.

Real-Life Example: Sandeep's Emotional Growth

Sandeep learned to recognize his girlfriend's emotional needs by enhancing his emotional intelligence. His ability to empathize and communicate effectively made their bond stronger and more fulfilling. Sandeep's commitment to emotional growth transformed his relationship and made him a more supportive and understanding partner. This example highlights the importance of emotional intelligence in building a deep and lasting connection.

Case Study: Rajat's Resilience and Ambition

Rajat's dedication to his writing career, even through tough times, made his partner admire him for his resilience and ambition. Rajat's passion for his work inspired his partner and added a sense of purpose to their relationship. This example demonstrates how staying passionate about your dreams can make you more attractive and inspiring.

Maintaining Her Interest Over Time

Winning her heart is just the beginning; keeping her interested requires continued effort. Relationships thrive when you consistently show appreciation, surprise her with exciting moments, and demonstrate your love and support.

Tips to Keep Her Interested:

1. Continue to Surprise Her: Plan new experiences and memorable moments. Keeping the spark alive requires effort and creativity. Whether it's a spontaneous date or a thoughtful gesture, surprises keep the relationship exciting.

2. Maintain Healthy Boundaries: Respect her individuality and personal space. Being supportive without being overly controlling makes her feel appreciated and valued. Healthy boundaries create a sense of trust and mutual respect.

3. Keep Growing: Never become stagnant in your personal growth. Continuously work on becoming a better version of yourself. Your commitment to self-improvement will inspire her and keep the relationship dynamic.

4. Express Appreciation: Never take her presence for granted. Genuine gratitude and acknowledgment of her efforts go a long way. Small gestures of appreciation, like a heartfelt compliment or a thoughtful note, make her feel valued.

5. Communicate Your Feelings: Regularly share your emotions and intentions with her. Open communication builds trust and intimacy. Being honest and vulnerable creates a deeper emotional connection.

Case Study: Ajay's Spontaneous Getaways

Ajay made it a tradition to plan spontaneous weekend getaways for him and his girlfriend. These trips kept their relationship vibrant and exciting, creating lasting memories and strengthening their bond. Ajay's effort to surprise his partner with new experiences kept the spark alive and made their relationship more fulfilling. This example highlights the importance of creativity and effort in maintaining a relationship.

Real-Life Example: Ramesh's Respect for Personal Space

Ramesh respected his girlfriend's need for personal time, which enhanced her appreciation for his understanding and maturity. Ramesh's ability to maintain healthy boundaries created a sense of trust and mutual respect in their relationship. This example demonstrates how respecting individuality can strengthen a relationship.

Case Study: Sameer's Journey of Self-Improvement

Sameer's journey of self-improvement not only benefited his own growth but also inspired his partner to do the same. Sameer's commitment to personal development created a sense of mutual support and encouragement in their relationship. This example illustrates how continuous growth can enhance both personal and relationship dynamics.

Real-Life Example: Vikrant's Thoughtful Gestures

Vikrant's habit of expressing appreciation through simple gestures like handwritten notes made his girlfriend feel deeply valued. Vikrant's consistent effort to show gratitude strengthened their emotional connection and made their relationship more fulfilling. This example highlights the power of appreciation in maintaining a strong bond.

Case Study: Suraj and Meera's Open Communication

Suraj and Meera's relationship grew stronger when Suraj learned to communicate his thoughts and feelings openly. Their ability to share their emotions and intentions fostered deeper understanding and connection. This example demonstrates how open communication can transform a relationship.

Conclusion:

Becoming the man she can't resist is about being your best self, enhancing your natural strengths, and consistently growing. The key is authenticity, confidence, kindness, and passion. When you project these qualities effortlessly, you'll be the man she not only desires but deeply values and respects. Personal growth is a lifelong journey that requires dedication, effort, and self-awareness. By continuously improving yourself, maintaining her interest, and fostering a deep emotional connection, you can create a relationship that is both fulfilling and enduring. Remember, the most attractive quality you can possess is the willingness to grow and evolve, not just for her but for yourself. When you prioritize personal growth, you become a man who is truly irresistible.

Chapter 13: Practical Tips and Real-Life Examples for Impressing Women

Introduction

Impressing women is an art that combines authenticity, confidence, and emotional intelligence. While there's no one-size-fits-all formula, understanding the principles of attraction and learning from real-life experiences can significantly improve your approach. This chapter delves into stories of successful and unsuccessful attempts to impress women, lessons learned from real-world experiences, expert tips from relationship psychologists, and final thoughts on being yourself and attracting women naturally. By the end of this chapter, you'll have a comprehensive guide to navigating the complexities of attraction and building meaningful connections.

Stories of Successful and Unsuccessful Attempts to Impress Women

Successful Attempts:

1. The Power of Genuine Compliments:

Story: Raj noticed that his colleague, Priya, had been working tirelessly on a project. Instead of making a generic compliment, he said, "I'm really impressed by how you handled the challenges in this project. Your dedication and problem-solving skills are inspiring." Priya appreciated the thoughtful compliment, and it sparked a deeper connection between them.

Lesson: Specific, genuine compliments show that you're paying attention and value her efforts.

2. Creating Memorable Experiences:

Story: Arjun planned a surprise picnic for his girlfriend, complete with her favorite food, a playlist of songs they both loved, and a scenic location. The effort and thoughtfulness behind the gesture made her feel cherished and special.

Lesson: Thoughtful gestures and shared experiences create lasting memories and deepen emotional bonds.

3. Active Listening and Empathy:

Story: When Meera shared her struggles with work-life balance, Rohan listened attentively without interrupting. He empathized with her situation and offered supportive advice. Meera felt understood and valued, which strengthened their relationship.

Lesson: Active listening and empathy are powerful tools for building trust and emotional intimacy.

Unsuccessful Attempts:

1. Overdoing Grand Gestures:

Story: Ankit planned an elaborate surprise party for his crush, inviting all her friends and family. However, she felt overwhelmed and uncomfortable with the attention, leading to an awkward situation.

Lesson: Grand gestures can backfire if they don't align with her preferences. Always consider her comfort level.

2. Trying Too Hard to Impress:

Story: Vikram constantly bragged about his achievements and material possessions during his date with Neha. Instead of being impressed, Neha found his behavior arrogant and self-centered.

Lesson: Authenticity is more attractive than trying too hard to impress. Focus on building a genuine connection.

3. Ignoring Her Boundaries:

Story: Aman insisted on paying for everything during his date with Shreya, even though she preferred to split the bill. His insistence made her feel uncomfortable and disrespected.

Lesson: Respect her boundaries and preferences. Pushing too hard can create discomfort and distance.

Lessons Learned from Real-World Experiences

1. Authenticity Wins:

Trying to be someone you're not is unsustainable and often leads to disappointment. Women appreciate men who are genuine and true to themselves.

2. Thoughtfulness Matters:

Small, thoughtful gestures often have a greater impact than grand, over-the-top displays of affection. It's the effort and sincerity behind the gesture that counts.

3. Communication is Key:

Open, honest communication is the foundation of any successful relationship. Misunderstandings often arise from poor communication, so make an effort to express yourself clearly and listen actively.

4. Respect Her Individuality:

Every woman is unique, with her own preferences, boundaries, and values. Respecting her individuality and understanding her needs is crucial for building a strong connection.

5. Consistency Builds Trust:

Trust is built through consistent actions and behaviors. Being reliable, dependable, and true to your word shows that you're someone she can count on.

Tips from Relationship Experts and Psychologists

1. Dr. John Gottman on Emotional Connection:

Tip: "Building emotional connection requires small, consistent acts of kindness and understanding. It's about creating a safe space where both partners feel valued and heard."

2. Esther Perel on Passion and Mystery:

Tip: "Maintaining a sense of mystery and excitement is essential for keeping the spark alive. Don't reveal everything at once; let her discover your layers over time."

3. Gary Chapman on Love Languages:

Tip: "Understanding her love language—whether it's words of affirmation, acts of service, receiving gifts, quality time, or physical touch—can help you express your love in a way that resonates with her."

4. Brené Brown on Vulnerability:

Tip: "Vulnerability is the birthplace of connection. Being open and honest about your feelings and fears creates a deeper emotional bond."

5. Susan David on Emotional Agility:

Tip: "Emotional agility—the ability to navigate your emotions with flexibility and resilience—is key to building strong, healthy relationships."

Final Thoughts on Being Yourself and Attracting Women Naturally

1. Embrace Your Authentic Self:

The most attractive quality you can possess is authenticity. Be true to yourself, and the right woman will appreciate you for who you are.

2. Focus on Personal Growth:

Continuous self-improvement not only makes you more attractive but also enhances your confidence and self-worth. Strive to be the best version of yourself.

3. Build Emotional Intelligence:

Understanding and managing your emotions, as well as empathizing with hers, is crucial for building a deep and lasting connection.

4. Create Shared Experiences:

Shared experiences create memories and strengthen your bond. Whether it's traveling together, trying new activities, or simply spending quality time, these moments build emotional intimacy.

5. Be Patient and Persistent:

Building a meaningful connection takes time and effort. Be patient, stay persistent, and don't be discouraged by setbacks.

6. Respect and Appreciate Her:

Show genuine respect and appreciation for her individuality, efforts, and presence in your life. Small gestures of gratitude go a long way in making her feel valued.

7. Communicate Openly and Honestly:

Open, honest communication is the foundation of any successful relationship. Share your thoughts, feelings, and intentions, and encourage her to do the same.

8. Maintain a Positive Attitude:

Positivity is contagious and attractive. Approach life with optimism and enthusiasm, and it will naturally draw people toward you.

9. Be Supportive and Encouraging:

Support her dreams, ambitions, and personal growth. Be her biggest cheerleader and show genuine interest in her success.

10. Stay True to Your Values:

Don't compromise your values or beliefs to impress someone. A strong sense of self and integrity is highly attractive.

Conclusion:

Impressing women is not about following a set of rules or tricks; it's about being your authentic self, building emotional connections, and continuously growing as a person. By learning from real-life experiences, incorporating expert advice, and staying true to your values, you can create meaningful and lasting relationships. Remember, the most attractive quality you can possess is the willingness to grow, evolve, and connect on a deeper level. When you prioritize authenticity, kindness, and emotional intelligence, you become a man who is not only impressive but also deeply respected and valued.

www.ingramcontent.com/pod-product-compliance
Ingram Content Group UK Ltd.
Pitfield, Milton Keynes, MK11 3LW, UK
UKHW021343190726
13845UKWH00027B/692

9 789334 262230